Pearson's Canal Comp[...]
SEVERN & AV[...]
GLOUCESTER & SHARPNESS, COTSWOLD CANALS, UPPER THAMES

Published by Central Waterways Supplies
of Rugby, Warwickshire
Tel/fax 01788 546692
email: sales@centralwaterways.co.uk
Copyright: Michael Pearson
All rights reserved
Sixth edition 2006
ISBN 0 9549116 5 2
ISBN-13 978-0-9-5491165-2

Tillerman

Boating up the Avon on behalf of my adoring public, a flashback came bubbling up from the murky depths of my memory bank. I was in a Landrover with the late David Hutchings, bumping down a rutted track at breakneck speed, covering a story for *Waterways World* concerning one of his perennially mutinous weirs. It was the only time I met him face to face, but I also rubbed shoulders with his boon companion Felix Pearson; and when Keith Goss came to do some research for a previous edition of this guide, David sent his regards and his appreciation, which, as far as I was concerned, was like receiving felicitations from an archangel.

David Hutchings did everything quickly - because there was so much to do. I liked to think that he was Andrew Yarranton reincarnated; Yarranton being the 17th Century polymath responsible for rendering a number of midland waterways navigable well in advance of Brindley and his contemporaries. They - or should that be 'he'? - were characterised by the sort of abrasive, self-absorbed zeal which 'gets things done' but which often antagonises the massed ranks of the organizationally and institutionally disposed. In the 21st Century it becomes increasingly difficult for such individuals to prosper. One imagines at that a Yarranton or Hutchings in their prime would have driven restoration of the Cotswold Canals through in the blink of an eye, leading manically from the front in a souped-up JCB. In reality, dates for completion are deferred, and, researching this edition it was sobering to discover that comparatively little advancement had been made since 2003, at which time it had confidently been predicted that completion of both the Stroudwater and Thames & Severn canals might be expected by 2010. Melancholically, now one senses that this is more likely to be a long drawn out Montgomery restoration scenario rather than a quickfire Rochdale or Huddersfield, and cynically one concludes that had it been a question of building a new road through the beautiful Frome Valley, progress would have been decidedly swifter. But better to cherish than be churlish, and the canals and navigable rivers in this guide are as beautiful as anything Britain has to offer. Get out there and explore them, and in doing so demonstrate, in the most effective of all manners, just how valuable waterways are to the country's sense of well-being, and just how wise and worthwhile investment in them can prove. I have been compiling these guides for quarter of a century, but my contribution seems small beer in comparison to activists like David Hutchings to the memory of whom this edition is humbly dedicated.

Michael Pearson

Karen Tanguy

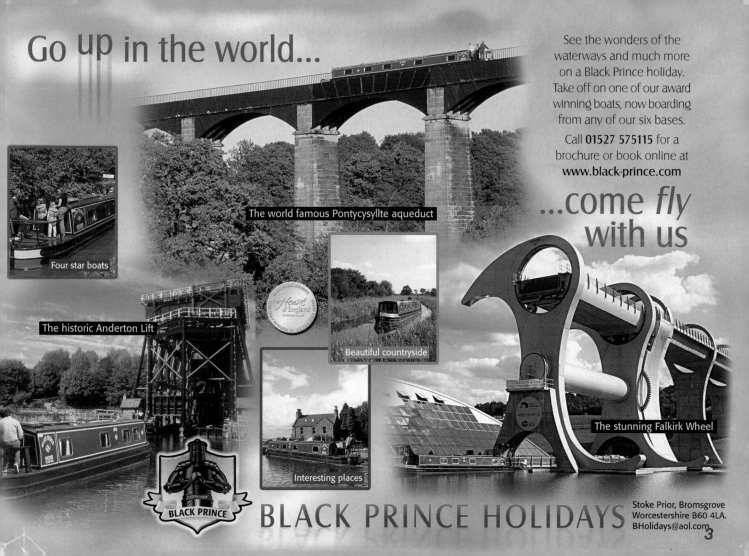

Go **up** in the world...

See the wonders of the waterways and much more on a Black Prince holiday. Take off on one of our award winning boats, now boarding from any of our six bases.

Call **01527 575115** for a brochure or book online at **www.black-prince.com**

...come *fly* with us

The world famous Pontycysyllte aqueduct

Four star boats

The historic Anderton Lift

Beautiful countryside

The stunning Falkirk Wheel

Interesting places

BLACK PRINCE

BLACK PRINCE HOLIDAYS

Stoke Prior, Bromsgrove Worcestershire B60 4LA. BHolidays@aol.com

3

UK-BOATINGholidays

If you are looking for a boating holiday you need look no further

 Hire direct from the leading narrowboat operators with all boats inspected and awarded star ratings by Visit Britain.

A fleet of over 180 boats for 2 to 12 people from 11 start bases throughout the UK so you can be sure of the widest choice.

Beginners are welcome

Visit our website or telephone for a free brochure pack.

08701 217 670

www.uk-boating.com

The River Avon

Sunrise, Bidford

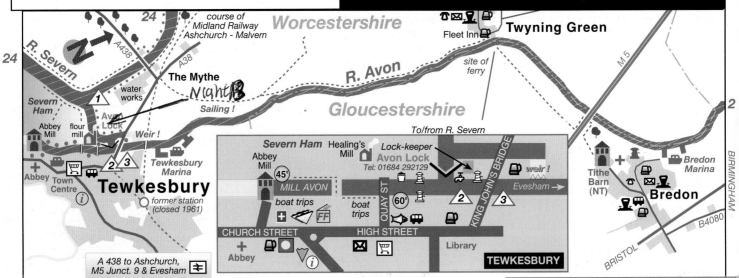

Worcestershire

course of
Midland Railway
Ashchurch - Malvern

R. Severn

24

The Mythe

water works

R. Avon

Fleet Inn — Twyning Green

site of ferry

Severn Ham

Sailing !

Gloucestershire

Abbey Mill — flour mill — Avon Lock

Weir !

Tewkesbury Marina

Abbey — Town Centre

Tewkesbury

former station (closed 1961)

A 438 to Ashchurch, M5 Junct. 9 & Evesham

To/from R. Severn

Severn Ham — Healing's Mill

Abbey Mill — 45'

Lock-keeper Avon Lock
Tel: 01684 292129

MILL AVON

boat trips

QUAY ST — 60'

boat trips

CHURCH STREET

HIGH STREET

Abbey

Library

weir !

Evesham →

KING JOHN'S BRIDGE

2   3

TEWKESBURY

Bredon Marina

Tithe Barn (NT)

Bredon

BIRMINGHAM

B4080

BRISTOL

M5

TEWKESBURY'S waterways may appear complex and disconcerting to the uninitiated: for instead of being content with one confluence with the Severn, the Avon branches into two channels. The main navigation passes through AVON LOCK and meets the Severn below Mythe Bridge, whilst the 'Mill Avon' flows between the back of the town and the open pastures of The Ham, being navigable as far as the ancient and picturesque Abbey Mill. However, for visiting boaters Avon Lock serves as the 'gateway to the river'. During working hours it is manned, and operated mechanically, by representatives of the Lower Avon Navigation Trust, who are normally prepared to dispense liberal quantities of local information and advice; they will certainly help you find a mooring (the best facilities being located on the Mill Avon between King John's Bridge and Healing's Mill) and may even try and sell you something from their range of souvenirs. LANT deserves your support, for without them there would be *no* navigable Avon.

Advice for Boaters

1. Entering or leaving the Avon from or for the Severn it is important to avoid the sandbar. Give this a wide berth by keeping over towards the southern bank as you turn into the Avon, and by making sure that Mythe Bridge is in view before turning upstream into the Severn.
2. Travelling downstream you may have to wait until Avon Lock is free for your use. Try to avoid being taken past the lock entrance by the current.
3. Use the largest arch only at King John's Bridge, and proceed carefully for visibility of oncoming craft is restricted.

Tewkesbury's waterfront is a delight. So many scenes catch the eye: the ancient arches of King John's Bridge; the quiet backwaters of the mill stream reflecting half-timbered houses and the town's towering abbey; and a pair of Healing's barges berthed against the dusty red-brick flour mill, vessels which look as if their sorties down to Sharpness or Avonmouth for the collection of grain are a thing of the past. A nearby bench commemorates William John (or 'Jack') Hitchman, one of Healings's former skippers.

Leaving Tewkesbury - however reluctantly - in your wake, you soon find yourself lost in a timeless landscape of lush watermeadows. The M5 motorway intrudes briefly, and noisily, into the river's secret world, before disappearing as rapidly as it arrived. And how delightfully intimate and cosy the Avon seems if you have come off the mighty Severn. How elevated your view of things, now that there are no high banks to hide the outside world. The riverside villages of Twyning and Bredon - well nigh impossible to visit by boat - are in different counties because this reach of the Avon forms the boundary between Gloucestershire and Worcestershire.

Tewkesbury (Map 1)

The radiant abbey of St Mary's looms maternally over the tumbling roofs of tight-knit streets, alleyways and courtyards which lead, at dizzy intervals, to tantalizing glimpses of boats moored on the Mill Avon: when the bells ring out for evensong it is easy to imagine that the centuries have rolled back to more god-fearing times. Tewkesbury was the fictional 'Elmbury' of John Moore's *Brensham Trilogy*, glorious post-war portraits of a Gloucestershire market town and its hinterland. Once you've tired of the town itself, there are some bracing walks to be enjoyed around the Severn Ham.

Eating & Drinking

BERKELEY ARMS - Church Street. Tel: 01684 293034. 16th century inn serving Wadworth, Badger and guest ales. Good food and a ghost! CAMRA recommended. AUBERGINE - Church Street. Tel: 01684 292703. Intimate restaurant.
MY GREAT GRANDFATHERS - Church Street. Tel: 01684 292687. Homely licenced restaurant.
ROYAL HOP POLE - Church Street. Tel: 01684 293236. Hotel (which Dickens booked Mr Pickwick into) offering bar and restaurant food together with limited moorings on the Mill Avon.
OLDE BLACK BEAR - High Street. Tel: 01684 292202) Possibly the oldest inn in Gloucestershire: pleasant riverside garden. *Also lots of ethnic restaurants & takeaways, plus three good fish & chip shops.*

Shopping

A lovely town to shop in, but do beware the narrow pavements and traffic which appears reluctant to take prisoners. 1471 (named after the battle, you know) is an admirable delicatessen on Church Street; a good place to head for when making up picnics. DAVID DUDLEY provides locally reared meat on Barton Street. ALISON'S BOOKSHOP on High Street is an excellent example of how an independent bookseller can thrive and they have a nice line in classical music as well. Almost next door is CORNELL BOOKS (alongside Barclays Bank) who are especially strong on topography and old OS mapping. But if it's more mundane merchandise that you're seeking, there are Tesco and Somerfield supermarkets. Market days are Wednesday and Saturday, and there's a Farmers Market on the second Saturday in the month. Finally, there's a launderette by the Town Cross.

Things to Do

TOURIST INFORMATION - Barton Street. Tel: 01684 295027. Small admission charge for adjoining museum of local history.
JOHN MOORE COUNTRYSIDE MUSEUM - Church Street. Tel: 01684 297174. Admission charge. Open Tue-Sat plus Bank Holidays.
TEWKESBURY ABBEY - Church Street. Tel: 01684 273736. Open daily. The visitor's centre features displays and exhibitions, as well as a refectory overlooking the abbey grounds.

Connections

BUSES - Service 41 links Tewkesbury with Cheltenham at frequent intervals calling en route at Ashchurch railway station. Upton, Gloucester, Malvern and Evesham are also served. Tel: 0870 608 2 608.
TRAINS - Ashchurch (for Tewkesbury) station lies 2 miles east. Tel: 08457 484950.
TAXIS - Avonside. Tel: 01684 292580.

Twyning Green & Bredon (Map 1)

Villages both devoid of public moorings. You can visit Twyning Green (complete with general stores and huge village green) however, by patronising the THE FLEET INN (Tel: 01684 274310) which has moorings for customers.

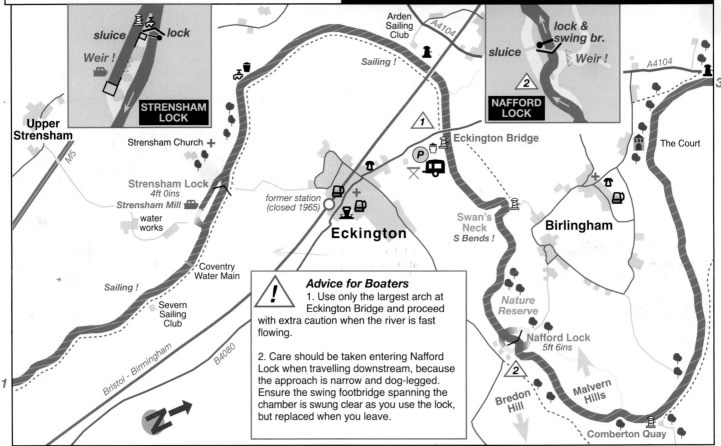

STRENSHAM LOCK

sluice — lock

Weir !

NAFFORD LOCK

sluice — lock & swing br.

Weir !

Upper Strensham

Strensham Church

Strensham Lock
4ft 0ins
Strensham Mill
water works

Coventry Water Main

Severn Sailing Club

Sailing !

Bristol - Birmingham

B4080

former station (closed 1965)

Eckington

Arden Sailing Club

A4104

Sailing !

P Eckington Bridge

Swan's Neck
S Bends !

Birlingham

The Court

A4104

Nature Reserve

Nafford Lock
5ft 6ins

Bredon Hill

Malvern Hills

Comberton Quay

Advice for Boaters

1. Use only the largest arch at Eckington Bridge and proceed with extra caution when the river is fast flowing.

2. Care should be taken entering Nafford Lock when travelling downstream, because the approach is narrow and dog-legged. Ensure the swing footbridge spanning the chamber is swung clear as you use the lock, but replaced when you leave.

By-road to The Combertons

Comberton village

THE Lower Avon seems infatuated by Bredon Hill, never letting it out of its sight, fascinated by the summit's constantly changing shape. Half wooded, half bare, like mottled baize, it forms an island between the Cotswold Edge and the distant serrated outline of the Malvern Hills. Because its peak falls short of a thousand feet, some 18th century eccentric built a folly on its top so that he could stand that high above sea level. But what are a few feet here or there in countryside as delectable as this? Each entertaining curve in the Avon reveals a new perspective, as if you are falling deeper and deeper in love with someone who is going to mean an awful lot to you.

This Avon is second only to the Thames in the amount of writing it has inspired, and this stretch is particularly rich in literary associations. Every guidebook quotes A. E. Housman's poem *In Summertime on Bredon* (an odd geographical aberration for a set of poems entitled *A Shropshire Lad*), but a better poem was written by Sir Arthur Quiller-Couch about Eckington Bridge. 'Q' had canoed the river as a young man in 1890, and had been inspired to compose a magnificent ode to the bridge which speaks of 'eloquent grooves worn into the sandstone by labouring bargemen'. Quiller-Couch also employed the river in his adventurous tale *True Tilda*, painting an especially evocative scene of the bustling barges and steam tugs at Tewkesbury. Following his own journey down the river in 1910, Temple Thurston used Nafford Mill (destroyed by fire in 1909) as the setting for his Richard Furlong trilogy, now long-forgotten and out of print, but still wonderful reading if you can find them (as it is reasonably easy to do) second-hand. It is not difficult to see why such writers were moved to capture the spirit of this quintessentially English landscape. It would be one of life's missed opportunities, were you not to moor, at Comberton Quay or Eckington Bridge, make an ascent of Bredon Hill, and see for yourself Housman's 'coloured counties' and *your* river, meandering through this peerless panorama like a wandering minstrel.

STRENSHAM LOCK is sometimes manned by volunteers. Being separated from the M5 by a church-topped hill (the tower of which is curiously cream-washed), it could be a million miles from the motorway service area that shares its name. Either side of the lock the river roams attractively past shallow banks of reeds and lily-pads rutted by cattle and sheep intent on quenching their thirst.

Bredon Hill

Downstream of Eckington's marvellously medieval bridge, in a reach plied by sailing craft from the Arden club, the busy Bristol-Derby railway crosses the river by way of a not ungraceful iron span resting on stone piers. It comes as something of a surprise to learn that Herbert Spencer, the influential Victorian philosopher, was instrumental in its design during a youthful sojourn in the engineering offices of the Birmingham & Gloucester Railway Company.

ENTRENCHED in the Vale of Evesham, the Avon makes its stately way past Tiddesley Wood, where the famous Pershore 'Egg' plum was discovered growing wild in 1833. Pollarded willows and swaying poplars betray the river's course as it meanders towards the sturdy tower of Pershore Abbey.

The original bridge at Pershore dates from the 14th century and contrives to look even older. Military men have always had a love/hate relationship with bridges, and the Cavaliers tried to demolish this one as they escaped from the Battle of Worcester in 1651. Thankfully it stood its ground. Seemingly nothing could mar the charm of its setting or its own inherent beauty. Nothing, that is, until the motor car came along, demanding

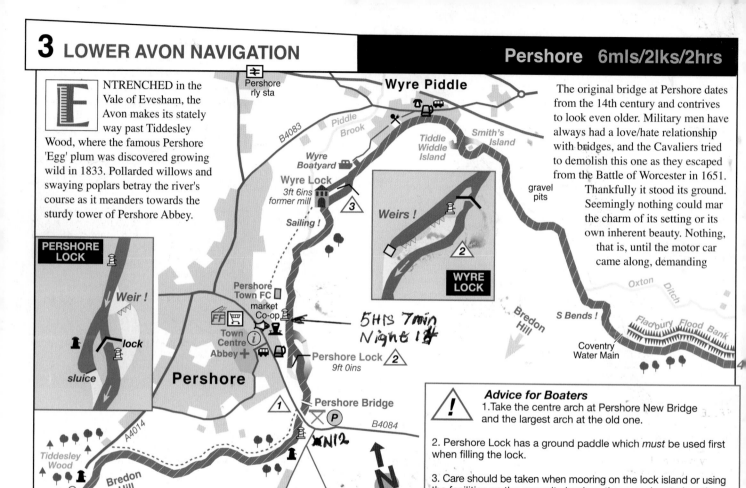

Advice for Boaters

1. Take the centre arch at Pershore New Bridge and the largest arch at the old one.

2. Pershore Lock has a ground paddle which *must* be used first when filling the lock.

3. Care should be taken when mooring on the lock island or using the facilities on the opposite bank as these are located on the weir channel. Also be aware of deflecting current from weirs at tail - compensate by angling bow towards flow.

construction of a straighter, flatter span. Built in 1928, it was the hailed as the first concrete bridge in Worcestershire, though sadly not the last. Pershore Mill was destroyed by fire in the early 1970s. It had been the last mill on the Avon in commercial use, and was also the river's last source of traffic. a little barge with the biblically appropriate name of *Pisgah* traded to and from the mill until the end.

WYRE LOCK is diamond shaped: many of the original Avon locks were of unusual configuration to reduce erosion of the chambers by the force of water from the sluices. Both the Lower and now Upper Avon Navigation Trusts have offices and workshops located in the old mill at Wyre. Desirable residences create an enviable riverside environment for the villagers of Wyre Piddle, but upstream the river soon loses itself amongst the fruit fields and orchards of this fertile valley. Herons and kingfishers abound. Time hangs motionlessly over the landscape like the cobwebby pendulum of an unwound grandfather clock. Fladbury flood bank dates from 1881. Four feet high, it has sluice valves built into its bank to protect the farmlands from the ravages of the river. The flood bank hasn't always been up to its task, as several high water marks in Fladbury village testify.

Pershore (Map 3)

Balconies blossoming from Georgian houses lend a holiday feel, an inherent *joie de vivre* to Pershore, best known nowadays, not for pears as the name implies, but for rich, ruby red plums. The Abbey, only marginally less imposing than Tewkesbury's, was only partially demolished following the Dissolution of the Monasteries. John Betjeman wrote of the abbey bells being rung for evensong in a poem called *Pershore Station*. Boaters are afforded easy access to the town centre over playing fields (and the imposing premises of Pershore Town FC '88') and past an impressive leisure centre (which contains a tempting swimming pool) beside a quaint and bustling indoor market.

Eating & Drinking

BELLE HOUSE TRAITEUR - Bridge Street. Tel: 01386 555055. Stylish modern restaurant/bar.
BRANDY CASK - Bridge Street. Tel: 01386 552602. Time-warp interior, gorgeous garden with hungry carp and limited customer moorings. Lovely home-brewed beer plus guests. Wholesome budget-priced food.
WHISTLERS - Broad Street. Tel: 01386 556900

Pershore Balconies

Amiable first floor bistro overlooking the sweep of Broad Street. Balcony tables for clement days. *There are also Thai and Indian restaurants and a plethora of fast food outlets (including traditional fish & chips) to be easily found by turning left on reaching the High Street.*

Shopping

Many boaters venture no further than the sizeable Co-op supermarket adjacent to the riverside recreation ground, but it would be a shame to miss out on the many antique and book shops sprinkled liberally around the town. A surprising find is SHERRIFF'S little fishmongery on Church Street: there are also a butcher, baker, two delicatessens and a launderette. The indoor retail market operates Wednesday through Saturday and oozes with small town atmosphere.

Things to Do

TOURIST INFORMATION - Town Hall, High Street. Tel: 01386 556591.

Connections

BUSES - Services to/from Worcester and Evesham. Tel: 0870 608 2 608.
TRAINS - Cotswold Line services by First Great Western Tel: 08457 484950.
TAXIS - Rod's Taxis. Tel: 01386 555285.

Wyre Piddle (Map 3)

Straggling but affluent village on the road between Pershore and Evesham. Shopless, Wyre Piddle is perhaps best known for the popular ANCHOR INN - Tel: 01386 556059 - but sustenance and moorings are also available at the adjoining AVONSIDE HOTEL - Tel: 01386 552654.

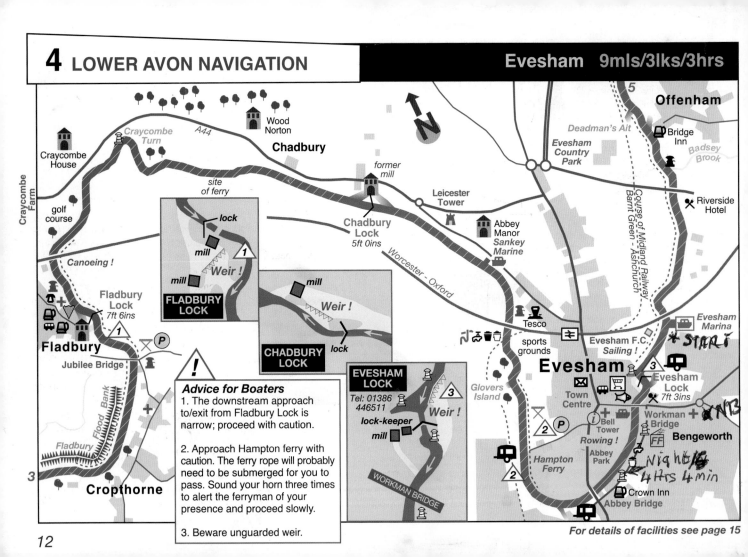

Offenham

Craycombe Turn

Wood Norton

Chadbury

Craycombe House

A44

Deadman's Ait

Evesham Country Park

Bridge Inn

Badsey Brook

Craycombe Farm

golf course

site of ferry

former mill

Leicester Tower

Riverside Hotel

Canoeing !

lock

mill

Weir !

FLADBURY LOCK

Chadbury Lock
5ft 0ins

Abbey Manor
Sankey Marine

Course of Midland Railway
Barnt Green - Ashchurch

Fladbury Lock
7ft 6ins

mill

Weir !

CHADBURY LOCK

lock

Worcester - Oxford

Tesco

sports grounds

Evesham Marina

★ START

Evesham F.C.
Sailing !

Fladbury

Jubilee Bridge !

P

!

Advice for Boaters
1. The downstream approach to/exit from Fladbury Lock is narrow; proceed with caution.

2. Approach Hampton ferry with caution. The ferry rope will probably need to be submerged for you to pass. Sound your horn three times to alert the ferryman of your presence and proceed slowly.

3. Beware unguarded weir.

EVESHAM LOCK
Tel: 01386 446511
lock-keeper
mill

Glovers Island

Weir !

3

Evesham Lock
7ft 3ins

FINISH

Evesham

Town Centre

Bell Tower

Rowing !

Workman Bridge

FF

Bengeworth

Flood Bank

Fladbury

Cropthorne

WORKMAN BRIDGE

Hampton Ferry

Abbey Park

Nights 16
4 Hrs 4 min

Crown Inn

Abbey Bridge

For details of facilities see page 15

EVESHAM marks the frontier between the Lower and Upper navigable sections of the River Avon. Between Cropthorne and Offenham the river practically boxes the compass on its gorgeous meanderings through the fruity vale.

In the 19th century the only way to cross the river at Cropthorne was to ford it. But in Queen Victoria's Jubilee year a bridge was built to span the river here, so that Fladbury lads could go courting Cropthorne lasses without necessarily getting their feet wet. One of the river's last working water-gates occupied the reach below Jubilee Bridge. These were devices for altering water levels without adversely affecting supplies to the mills. A conventional lock here would have lowered the water level to the detriment of the mill at Wyre. The water-gate provided a simple alternative. It consisted of a gate fitted with sluices set into a weir. In normal circumstances the gate would remain open until a boat passed through on its way upstream. Then the gate would be closed while the boat waited for a sufficient level of water to be built up to enable it to navigate up to Fladbury Lock. On the way back the sluices would be drawn on reaching the gate, and there a boat would wait until the levels had equalised and the gate could be opened. L. T. C. Rolt described its use in *Landscape With Machines*. He and his fiance, Angela, had hired a cabin cruiser called *Miranda* from a boatyard at Wyre Piddle in 1938 in order to 'test the water' prior to plunging into full time life afloat with *Cressy* as seminally related in his classic book *Narrow Boat*.

The Avon at Fladbury is the stuff of dreams. Once there were two mills, that beside the lock being known as Cropthorne Mill in deference to its position. It is linked to the outside world by a private rope ferry. The other, quite naturally, was called Fladbury Mill and in latter years a pair of Armfield 20hp turbines were installed to provide the village with electricity. Grandiosely known as the Fladbury Electric Light & Power Co., they charged ten shillings per light per annum to householders in the district.

The rhyming locks at Fladbury and Chadbury deserve a poem about them. Certainly there is plenty of inspiration in the landscape as the river winds past the orcharded flanks of Craycombe and Wood Norton. Craycombe House - guarded by a tall cedar - was built for George Perrott, an 18th century owner of the navigation. The novelist Francis Brett Young lived in it during the Thirties. Wood Norton Hall was ostentaciously erected in 1897 for the Duke of Orleans, pretender to the French throne. During the Second World War it became a BBC centre for radio monitoring of foreign stations, and quite possibly Hitler's death was first learned of here. In response to the Cold War a deep nuclear bunker was added: light entertainment for the survivors, perhaps? Following an ill-fated stint as a luxury hotel, the house is expected to be broken up into retirement flats. Chadbury Lock was the first to be rebuilt by LANT in 1953. Much of the work was done by the Royal Engineers, a pioneering use of military resources on a civilian project.

Above the treetops bordering the next reach stands the Leicester Tower, built in 1840 as a memorial to Simon de Montfort, the Earl of Leicester, who came a cropper at the Battle of Evesham in 1265. The monks of Evesham Abbey planted vineyards on these south-facing slopes in the Middle Ages. Now these selfsame slopes appear to belong entirely to something called TESCO! Round the corner two railway bridges spanned the river. One remains, carrying the highly scenic Cotswolds & Malverns line. The other, a victim of Beeching, carried the Midland Railway route from Redditch to Ashchurch near Tewkesbury. If it had remained open north of Evesham at least, it might have been more than a little useful as a commuter link with Birmingham today, a mere sixteen miles of railway permanently lost through dubiously reached and short-sighted, accountancy-led thinking. The abandoned abutments of the vanished bridge retain a latent dignity as exemplified by their ochre-coloured corner stones.

Glass houses, glinting in the sunlight, emphasise Evesham's reputation as a fruit growing centre, as the river skirts its western suburbs and you pass the flourishing ferry at HAMPTON. This is one of only two public ferries still in existence on the Avon. It provides a popular short cut for the housewives of Hampton to reach Evesham's shops. There is an aesthetic pleasure in its to-ing and fro-ing which makes you sad that not more of the

Cropthorne Mill, Fladbury

GOLDCREST
BIDFORD BOATS
01789·773205

14

river's ferries have survived. Local authorities, one feels, might have done more to preserve such operations, if only to maintain the integrity of public rights of way.

A stately bridge, named after one of the town's Victorian mayors, spans the Avon in the centre of EVESHAM, and recreation grounds, bordered by an avenue of limes, create a gracious riverside environment. On hot days, with Evesham en fete, you might be reminded of Seurat's pointillistic masterpiece of the Ile de la Grande-Jatte. Evesham Lock is the highest upstream on the Lower Avon. A triangular-shaped lock-keeper's house spans the original, long since disused chamber. Here, the paperwork and pleasantries, courtesies and formalities of a frontier are exchanged despite a recent melding of the two distinct navigation trusts' operations.

Between Evesham and OFFENHAM the river is left pretty much to its own devices. The railway and the by-pass cross the Avon but leave little impression on it. Beyond the watermeadows, and the likelihood of floods, the countryside is thick with regimented fruit trees and the ubiquitous green houses in which Evesham's reputation as a centre for the cultivation of tomato plants is forged.

Deadman's Ait was the scene of heavy fighting during the Battle of Evesham. Many Welshmen were slaughtered in the vicinity, and large quantities of human remains were unearthed during the eighteenth century. The peace we associate with the English landscape had to be fought for.

Fladbury (Map 4)

Alas and alack, the absence of suitable moorings renders the pretty village of Fladbury effectively beyond the reach of boaters - Temple Thurston would feel betrayed and Mrs Izod aghast that the ferry no longer operates for the benefit of the public and radish pickers. One becomes even more frustrated when one learns that THE CHEQUERS (Tel: 01386 860276) is an excellent inn offering good food, accommodation and locally-brewed beer, and that, though bereft of a general store, the village retains its butcher. Consolation can be found at CRAYCOMBE FARM, (accessible from the pleasant moorings at Craycombe Turn - but *do* take care of the traffic) which bills itself as a Rural Business & Retail Park. Tel: 01386 860473 *www.craycombefarm.com*

Evesham (Map 4)

One expects romantic things of Evesham, cynosure of its fruity vale, and at last the by-pass and pedestrianisation between them seem to have created a sense of calm that has been absent since the invention of the motor car. Highlights include: the Bell Tower, all that's left of an abbey demolished following the Dissolution. Compare its fate with Pershore, losing only its nave and Tewkesbury, surviving virtually intact. Time your visit to hear the tower's carillon - playing *Linden Lea* when we last passed.

Eating & Drinking

TRUMPET INN - Merstow Green. Heavenly Hook Norton & food virtually opposite the Tourist Information Centre. Tel: 01386 446227.
ASK - Vine Street. Stylish Italian in the town centre. Tel: 01386 424545.
THE LANTERN - Bridge Street. Highly retro cod & chips, omelettes etc. Tel: 01386 47726.
CROWN INN - adjacent Abbey Bridge. Tel: 01386 446151. Homely local offering bar and restaurant food plus accommodation. Banks's and Theakston's beers.
RIVERSIDE HOTEL - Hotel restaurant located a mile or so above Evesham Lock with limited moorings for customers. Tel: 01386 446200.
BRIDGE INN - riverside, Offenham. Tel: 01386 446565. Donnington beers from Stow-on-the-Wold, plus regular guests. Food daily and a nice setting beside the river.

Shopping

Bridge Street and High Street are the principal shopping thoroughfares, along with the River Side indoor shopping centre, the latter being the site for many of the well known chain stores including a branch of MARKS & SPENCER'S 'SIMPLY FOOD'. Also of note are the 'hot pork baps' from ROBFI'S deli and sandwich shop at the river end of High Street. But don't ignore Bengeworth, east of the river, which has a good bakery, a bike shop, launderette, pharmacy, heaps of takeaways, and a really excellent secondhand bookshop called BOOKWORMS (Tel: 01386 45509).

Things to Do

TOURIST INFORMATION - The Almonry, Abbey Gate. Tel: 01386 446944.
ALMONRY HERITAGE CENTRE - Abbey Gate. Tel: 01386 446944. Admission charge. The former home of the Abbey Almoner today houses a heritage centre detailing the history of the town.
BOAT HIRE - skiffs, motorboats and river trips - Tel: 07860 895416.

Connections

BUSES - Services to/from Pershore and Worcester (not Sundays). Tel: 01905 763888.
TRAINS - Cotswold Line services to/from Worcester, Pershore and Oxford by First Great Western. Tel: 08457 484950.
TAXIS - Tel: 01386 48414.

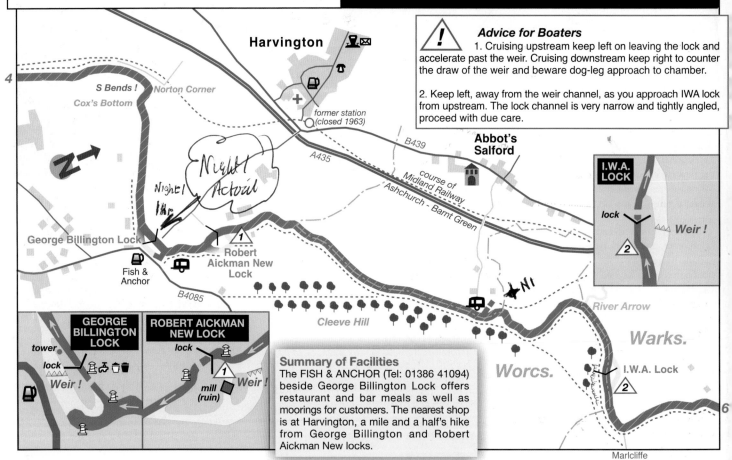

Harvington

Norton Corner

S Bends !

Cox's Bottom

4

former station (closed 1963)

A435

B439

Abbot's Salford

course of Midland Railway
Ashchurch - Barnt Green

Night Actual

Night 1hr

George Billington Lock

Fish & Anchor

B4085

⚠ 1
Robert Aickman New Lock

N1

Cleeve Hill

River Arrow

Warks.

Worcs.

I.W.A. Lock

⚠ 2

Marlcliffe

6

Advice for Boaters

1. Cruising upstream keep left on leaving the lock and accelerate past the weir. Cruising downstream keep right to counter the draw of the weir and beware dog-leg approach to chamber.

2. Keep left, away from the weir channel, as you approach IWA lock from upstream. The lock channel is very narrow and tightly angled, proceed with due care.

I.W.A. LOCK

lock

Weir !

⚠ 2

GEORGE BILLINGTON LOCK

tower

lock

Weir !

ROBERT AICKMAN NEW LOCK

lock

⚠ 1

mill (ruin)

Weir !

Summary of Facilities

The FISH & ANCHOR (Tel: 01386 41094) beside George Billington Lock offers restaurant and bar meals as well as moorings for customers. The nearest shop is at Harvington, a mile and a half's hike from George Billington and Robert Aickman New locks.

RIFTING through time and space, the Avon wends its secluded way between Evesham and Bidford. Substantially different in character to the lower river, the Upper Avon has a wilder feel to it, akin perhaps to the uppermost reaches of the River Thames between Oxford and Lechlade. It was appropriate, therefore, that second-hand paddle gear from Thames locks was used in the restoration of the Upper Avon. And what a mammoth undertaking it was, costing more than six times as much as the Lower Avon restoration project.

All the Upper Avon locks are named after individuals or groups associated with the restoration of the river. The work at GEORGE BILLINGTON LOCK was completed in just six weeks so that its donor, who was terminally ill in his thirties, might observe the effect of his benefaction before he died. ROBERT AICKMAN NEW LOCK commemorates one of the most influential figures of the post war inland waterways renaissance. Aickman founded the Inland Waterways Association in 1946 and crusaded for the waterways cause for a further twenty years. Returning navigation to the Avon was dear to his heart, and he was on the council of both Trusts. A memorial plaque, set in an attractive sweep of brickwork, graces the lockside, paying homage to his achievements and single-minded determination. More practically, the boater is thankful for the provision of free overnight moorings on most Upper Avon lock cuts, many located in blissfully remote rural surroundings. Sir Arthur Quiller-Couch wrote of 'clouds of sweet-smelling flour' issuing from the doorway of Cleeve Mill, but virtually all trace of the lock, weir and mill at Cleeve has vanished. Up until the Second World War this was a popular venue for picnics. You could get cream teas at the mill and hire a skiff for a leisurely row up the river. The Avon broadened below the weir and was shallow enough to be crossed by hay carts at harvest time. A correspondent from Canada wrote to tell us that his great uncle once lived in the mill, commuting from Salford Priors station to Birmingham, where he was the conductor of the symphony orchestra and on personal terms with Tchaikovsky:

Robert Aickman Memorial

what interesting people the Canal Companion readers are!

At the foot of its wooded escarpment, the setting at Cleeve remains seductive, though somewhat compromised by the presence now of a caravan park on the Warwickshire bank, and it is disappointing that boaters have no official access to the pretty village of Cleeve itself.

Downstream of the IWA LOCK, the River Arrow has its confluence with the Avon. Consideration was given to making this navigable in the 17th century, but nothing materialised. The Arrow rises on the Lickey Hills and passes through the lower reservoir at Bittell beside the Worcester & Birmingham Canal, so you may well see it again. Likewise its tributary, the Alne, which follows the Stratford Canal for a while in the vicinity of Preston Bagot.

Marlcliffe is aptly named, for the Trust had considerable problems during the construction of the IWA Lock, due to the unyielding quality of the substrata. UANT's handbook describes many of the difficulties overcome during the restoration in a matter of fact way, a modesty which fails to disguise the vast amount of work they undertook - and continue to undertake - on our behalf.

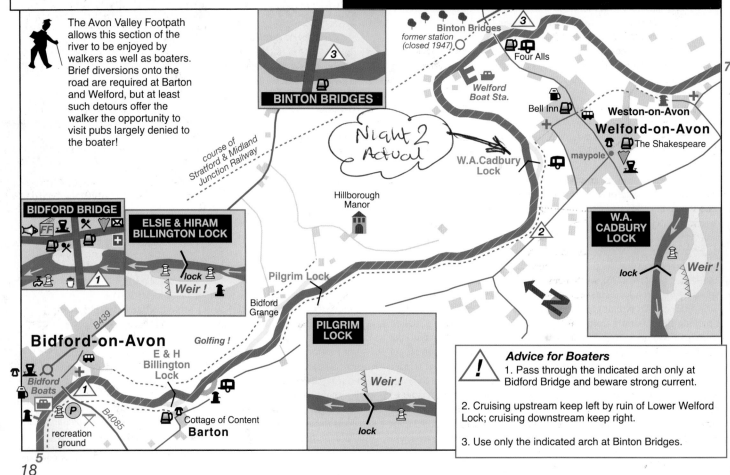

The Avon Valley Footpath allows this section of the river to be enjoyed by walkers as well as boaters. Brief diversions onto the road are required at Barton and Welford, but at least such detours offer the walker the opportunity to visit pubs largely denied to the boater!

BINTON BRIDGES

Binton Bridges

former station (closed 1947)

Four Alls

Welford Boat Sta.

Bell Inn

Weston-on-Avon

Welford-on-Avon

The Shakespeare

maypole

W.A.Cadbury Lock

course of Stratford & Midland Junction Railway

Night 2 Actual

Hillborough Manor

W.A. CADBURY LOCK

lock   Weir !

BIDFORD BRIDGE

ELSIE & HIRAM BILLINGTON LOCK

lock   Weir !

Pilgrim Lock

Bidford Grange

Bidford-on-Avon

E & H Billington Lock

Bidford Boats

recreation ground

B439

B4085

Golfing !

Cottage of Content **Barton**

PILGRIM LOCK

Weir !

lock

Advice for Boaters

1. Pass through the indicated arch only at Bidford Bridge and beware strong current.

2. Cruising upstream keep left by ruin of Lower Welford Lock; cruising downstream keep right.

3. Use only the indicated arch at Binton Bridges.

NARROW and winding - rather after the fashion of life itself - the Upper Avon is at its loveliest between Bidford and Weston. Like dividends from a sagaciously garnered investment portfolio, locks come at satisfying intervals, but the rest of the time you have every justification for just sitting back and watching the peaceful landscape slip uneventfully astern. BIDFORD positively bristles with boats, coming into moor with varying degrees of proficiency, or threading their way gingerly through the eye of a needle navigation arch of the 15th Century bridge. Old cronies gossip on the cutwaters, enjoying a private joke or two at the expense of the less adept boaters, or eyeing with obvious relish the amount of flesh exposed by female boaters on hot days.

The Romans elected to cross the Avon at Bidford. Their Ryknield Street forded the river here on its way to the town of Alcester. Later the road was known as Buckle Street, and it was the monks of Alcester who erected the present bridge which dates from 1482. None of its seven arches are alike in size or shape, and it still looks so medieval that the regular passage across the narrow span of lorries and double-decker buses looks ridiculously anachronistic.

The official moorings at Bidford provide sufficient space for only three or four narrowboats alongside the Recreation Ground. If there are no spaces left you could patronise the Frog & Bulrush pub which also offers limited moorings, see if Bidford Boats have any spare room, or try E&H Billington Lock which is linked by footpath to Bidford, a quarter of an hour's walk away.

UANT's locks are not always situated in exact accordance with those on the original navigation. For instance, E. & H. Billington and Pilgrim locks are located either side of the former lock at Bidford Grange. Similarly, there used to be separate locks at Welford which UANT replaced with the single W. A. Cadbury Lock. These changes were necessitated by the alteration of water levels in the intervening years between dereliction of the original navigation and the commencement of the new scheme in the early Seventies. The attitudes of landowners, local and water authorities also influenced the final shape of the UANT project. Sometimes such individuals were extraordinarily helpful, whilst others seemed determined to stop the scheme in its tracks. Inexplicably, as Robert Aickman put it, the restorers were not always seen to be on the side of the angels.

The river splits into several channels - only one of which is navigable - to pass beneath the ancient arches of BINTON BRIDGES. Nearby lies the trackbed of the old Stratford & Midland Junction Railway, one of those endearingly independent cross-country lines which seemed to lead from nowhere to nowhere. At plum-picking time as many as twenty wagons a day were loaded with fruit in the tiny siding at Binton. Amongst the line's best remembered trains were the banana specials operated by the Midland Railway between Avonmouth Docks and London; a somewhat elongated route.

Bidford-on-Avon (Map 6)

There is a resort-like air about Bidford. Day-trippers pour on to the riverside recreation ground but rarely stray further than the local pubs and fast food outlets. Moreover such over-indulgences fail to mar what is an otherwise attractive village. In any case, Shakespeare came here to debauch himself too, immortalising the place in one of his poems as 'drunken Bidford'.

Eating & Drinking

THE BRIDGE - Tel: 01789 773700. Riverside 'eaterie'; Les Routiers recommended with nice balconies overlooking the water and a thoughtfully considered menu.
FROG & BULRUSH - Tel: 01789 772369. Riverside pub offering bar and restuarant food and limited customer mooring space.
SPICE AVON - Tel: 01789 490888. Indian. *As befits a resort, there are plenty of fast food outlets in addition to the above.*

Shopping

More shops than most villages of this size can sustain: butcher, bakery, pharmacy, convenience store (with cash machine), newsagent, post office and even a branch of Lloyds TSB bank. BUDGENS supermarket on main road to rear of Bidford Boats.

Connections

BUSES - Services to/from Evesham, Stratford and Redditch. Tel: 0870 608 2 608.

Welford-on-Avon (Map 6)

Lack of public moorings prevents easy exploration of this pretty village complete with maypole, thatched cottages, general stores and butcher. The FOUR ALLS at Binton Bridges (Tel: 01789 750228) offers limited customer moorings, whilst there are two more pubs in the village itself: THE BELL (Tel: 01789 750353) and THE SHAKESPEARE (Tel: 01789 750443).

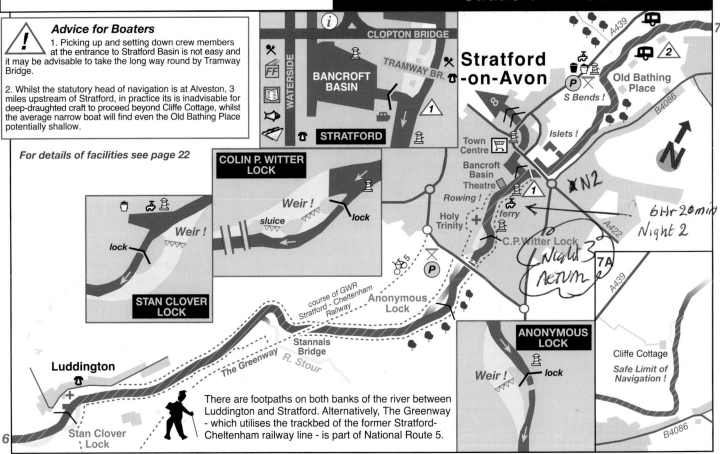

*Time refers to Luddington-Stratford and the lock count does not include access to Bancroft Basin.

BOATERS have three river locks to contend with (plus a fourth if they are moving on to or off the canal at Stratford) as the Upper Avon winds from Luddington, past Stratford, to the present head of navigation at Alveston Weir. Luddington Lock was renamed STAN CLOVER LOCK in 1997 in honour of one of UANT's loyal supporters. Boosted by the Stour, whose source lies near the brewery town of Hook Norton, the Avon widens perceptibly after the narrow reaches in the vicinity of Bidford. Above the confluence a large steel girder bridge carries the trackbed of the old Great Western Railway's Stratford-Cheltenham line. Now known as 'The Greenway', it stretches from Stratford to Long Marston, a useful escape route from the busy tourist town for walkers, cyclists and horse-riders. Andrew Yarranton proposed rendering the Stour navigable in the 17th Century. ANONYMOUS LOCK commemorates all those who donated funds towards restoration of the Upper Avon, including an individual who made the staggering donation of £100,000. Following his death in 1998, that individual has been revealed as one Charles Gray, who had made his fortune in the diamond mines of South Africa! The late Queen Mother travelled from here to the next lock up by narrowboat during the opening ceremony of June 1st 1974, as celebrated in the poem *Inland Waterway* by Sir John Betjeman.

The short reach separating Anonymous and Colin P. Witter locks is spanned by the Stratford & Midland Junction Railway bridge which was converted to carry road traffic. One of the last trains to cross over the river was the Royal Train, carrying the Queen Mother to officiate at the reopening of the Stratford Canal in 1964 - she obviously had a fondness for Stratford and its inland waterways! A footbridge also crosses the river at this point, making it easy for pedestrians to enjoy a circular walk beside the Avon. Blocks of highly desirable flats occupy the site of Lucy's Mill, which stood here for hundreds of years and was an important customer of the river barges until the advent of the railway.

Stratford New Lock was renamed COLIN P. WITTER LOCK in 1986. Massive steel frames protect the chamber from collapse threatened by high ground pressures. The bold steeple of Holy Trinity Church (Shakespeare's burial place) overlooks the lock, above which Stratford's passenger ferry boat operates by means of a submerged chain fed through a winch on the pontoon wound by the ferryman.

Stratford's riverfront is familiar to people from all over the world. Indeed, you are seemingly more likely to overhear the accents of New York or Tokyo than Warwickshire. And everyone seems determined to get afloat. Barnacle-encrusted navigators of the Avon Ring have to keep a weather-eye peeled for sudden unexpected and unpremeditated lurches to port or starboard; whilst, after all the day-trippers have departed, the reach becomes a training ground for the more accomplished performers of Stratford Rowing Club. A long river bank, backed by playing fields, extends between Colin P. Witter Lock and Tramway Bridge, providing an alternative, marginally less public berth to the canal basin, and on the opposite bank stands the Royal Shakespeare Theatre, currently undergoing a multi-million pound makeover. Upstream of the entrance lock to Stratford Basin the river is spanned by the TRAMWAY BRIDGE, a redbrick structure built in 1826 to carry the Stratford & Moreton Horse Tramway. It is now used by pedestrians. In contrast, the stone arches of CLOPTON BRIDGE date back to 1480. But the two bridges harmonise well with their shared environment, as though the gap of four centuries in their age was just a twinkling ripple in the timespan of the river beneath them.

Beyond Stratford it's feasible for most craft to voyage a further mile or so to the old Bathing Place, a picnic site provided with boating facilities, albeit on the shallow side for narrowboaters. The Upper Avon Navigation Trust have long advocated a bold scheme to extend navigation up to a junction with the Grand Union Canal at Radford Semele to the south of Leamington Spa. Ten locks and sixteen miles seem modest by the standards of many inland waterway project proposals, and the boost to tourism and the benefits of improved flood control are manifest, but the concept has so far foundered on the reactionary response of riparian landowners. Meanwhile, thanks to the continued work of the two Trusts and their volunteers, boaters have fifty miles of gorgeous river to play with. Attitudes and personalities change - the river can bide its time.

Stratford-on-Avon   *(Maps 7 & 8)*

That Stratford-on-Avon is second only to London in the esteem of foreign visitors, serves to emphasise the charisma surrounding Shakespeare. Without his omnipresence, one imagines Stratford's position in the league table of tourism would be academic. And yet, subtract the Shakespeare factor, and you are still left with an attractive town with a large helping of good architecture, its setting enhanced by the proximity of the Avon, and there is a hair-down demeanour about the people in the streets which becomes infectious. Contriving a dramatic analogy, Stratford delivers its lines and plays its part, but survives with its integrity and dignity intact, really being the rather nice place to visit as extolled by the tourist propaganda.

Eating & Drinking

GEORGETOWN - Sheep Street. Tel: 01789 204445. Colonial Malaysian cooking.

THE OPPO - Sheep Street. Tel: 01789 269980. Classy restaurant.

LAMBS - Sheep Street. Tel: 01789 292554. Ditto!

THE VINTNER - Sheep Street. Tel: 01789 297259. Ditto again!!

CAFE ROUGE - Sheep Street. Tel: 01789 263526. French chain.

BARNABY'S - Waterside. Tel: 01789 261485. Fish & chips, eat in or takeaway, handy for famished boaters.

QUARTO'S - Waterside. Tel: 01789 403415. Comfortable modern restaurant housed within Royal Shakespeare Theatre.

THE BOATHOUSE - riverside between Tramway and Clopton bridges. Tel: 01789 297733. Thai restaurant.

SHAKESPEARE HOTEL - Chapel Street. Fine beams, fine beer, fine food. Tel: 01789 294771.

EDWARD MOON - Chapel Street. Tel: 01789 267069. English brasserie.

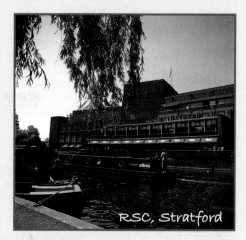

RSC, Stratford

HATHAWAYS - High Street. Tel: 01789 292404. Old-fashioned tearooms.

THISTLE HOTEL - Waterside. Bar and restaurant meals as well as a choice of real ales. Lovely garden for eating *al fresco*. Tel: 01789 294949.

Shopping

Market day is Friday and a good one it is too; plus Farmers' Markets on the first and third Saturdays of the month and craft markets on the second and fourth Saturdays. Elsewhere the town bristles with quality shops engaged in the hectic business of emptying the bank accounts of visitors. But many of these shops have such character that you don't resent being plunged into the red. Even the chain stores, like Marks & Spencer on Bridge Street, appear to have more flair than branches elsewhere. The best policy, chaps, is to get here after the shops have shut and insist on an early start. A 24 hour branch of TESCO stands within easy reach of Bridge 65 on the canal.

Things to Do

TOURIST INFORMATION - Bridgefoot. Tel: 0870 160 7930. Within a minute's walk - pelican crossing permitting - of Bancroft Basin.

CITY SIGHTSEEING - Open top bus tours providing a good introduction to the town's attractions. Charge. Tel: 01789 299123.

ROYAL SHAKESPEARE THEATRE - Waterside. Whatever else you do in Stratford, try to catch a performance at the RST, or at one of the two other theatres in town, The Swan or The Other Place. Tel: 0870 609 1110.

SHAKESPEARE'S BIRTHPLACE - Henley Street. Tel: 01789 201822. S's childhood home.

NASH'S HOUSE & NEW PLACE - Chapel Street. Tel: 01789 292325. S's grown-up home.

HALL'S CROFT - Old Town. Tel: 01789 292107. Home of S's daughter and her doctor husband.

SHAKESPEARIENCE - Waterside. Tel: 01789 290111. "Experience the genius of Shakespeare in just one hour!" *Don't you wish it had been that easy at A Level!*

SHAKESPEARE EXPRESS - Tel: 0121 708 4960. The Bard's favourite means of transport - steam hauled trains to Birmingham and back on Sundays in summer.

AVON-BOATING - Swan's Nest. Tel: 01789 267073. Skiff, punt, canoe and motor-boat hire plus river trips for those unfortunate enough to be without their own vessel.

Connections

BUSES - useful downriver links with Bidford-on-Avon and Evesham and up-canal connections with Wootton Wawen, Hockley Heath, Shirley et al. Tel: 0870 608 2 608.

TRAINS - Hourly services to Birmingham via Wootton Wawen and Henley-in-Arden. Less frequent but still useful direct link with London Marylebone by Chiltern Trains. Tel: 08457 484950.

TAXIS - Stratford Taxis. Tel: 01789 414007.

The Stratford Canal

Lock 36 near Preston Bagot

THE Stratford Canal holds a special place in the affections of a generation of canal enthusiasts, its southern section being the first great restoration success of the post-war canal movement. It was transformed from virtual dereliction and the threat of abandonment in 1958 to navigable status once again in 1964. The restoration project, managed by the indomitable David Hutchings, was undertaken under the aegis of the National Trust, but in 1988 ownership of the canal passed to British Waterways.

Little evidence survives of former commercial activity at Stratford Canal (or Bancroft) Basin. Ice cream boats, baguette boats, and a floating art gallery lend it nowadays a Disneyland ambience, though it remains an entertaining spot to moor; always assuming you are gregariously pre-disposed and able to find a space. Quieter canal moorings are to be had through Bridge 69, an unobtrusive exit from the basin which begins (or, of course, ends) exploration of the Stratford Canal, and the canal's traverse of the town's eastern outskirts, through a quartet of locks, is surprisingly anonymous; just like Rosencrantz and Guildenstern you might say.

Above the locks, a boatyard creates a sense of activity as the canal passes beneath two railway bridges (look out for Summer Sunday steam trains) and passes the town's little football stadium.

Well kept and easy to operate, WILMCOTE LOCKS, like Caesar's Gaul and strawberry cheesecake, are divided into three distinct parts: two outer threes and a middle five. For ease of maintenance and access to two canalside cottages, the status of the towpath here has been upgraded to that of a minor road.

BRIDGE 59 was the straw that almost broke the camel's back. Its deterioration caused the local authority to seek permission to abandon the canal back in 1958, so that they could divert the roadway across the bed of the waterway. Evidence as to the canal's use relied on the purchase of a solitary ticket for a canoe trip the previous year! The only real function that the canal performed at the time was as a source of water for the steam locomotives at Stratford engine shed. The canal narrows at the site of a former quarry and lime-burning wharf, and the abutments of an old tramway bridge recall this activity. Wilmcote boasts good moorings for visiting boaters.

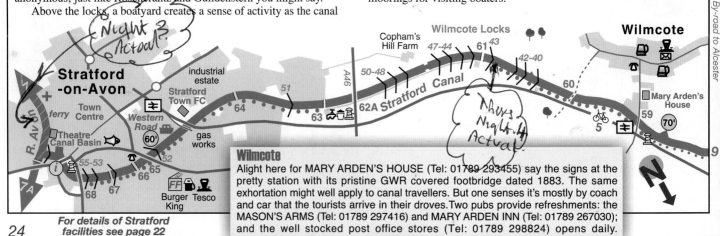

Wilmcote

Alight here for MARY ARDEN'S HOUSE (Tel: 01789 293455) say the signs at the pretty station with its pristine GWR covered footbridge dated 1883. The same exhortation might well apply to canal travellers. But one senses it's mostly by coach and car that the tourists arrive in their droves. Two pubs provide refreshments: the MASON'S ARMS (Tel: 01789 297416) and MARY ARDEN INN (Tel: 01789 267030); and the well stocked post office stores (Tel: 01789 298824) opens daily.

DD Lock separates two lengthy and delightfully remote pounds between the locks at Wilmcote and Preston Bagot. EDSTONE AQUEDUCT - sometimes known as Bearley - is undoubtedly the Stratford Canal's most dramatic engineering feature. It consists of an iron trough resting on thirteen tapering brick piers. At 28 feet high and 475 feet long, it seems modest enough, but in the context of the gently rolling landscape, its sudden appearance has the majesty and startling effect of the renowned Pontcysyllte Aqueduct on the Llangollen Canal. The sunken towpath offers walkers a strange, fish-eye lens view of passing boaters. The aqueduct spans a by-road, a tributary of the River Alne and the twin tracks of the Birmingham & North Warwickshire Railway whose undistinguished diet of diesel units is supplemented on Summer Sundays by the steam-hauled 'Shakespeare Express'. Those with a trained railway eye will notice an overgrown trackbed curving away from beneath the aqueduct across the countryside in a north-westerly direction. This was the Great Western Railway's Alcester branch, an ill-fated and relatively shortlived line which had its track lifted as an economy measure during the First World War, re-opened in 1923, then closed again at the beginning of the Second World War, apart from a semi-secret service operated for employees at a motor works evacuated from Coventry.

WOOTTON WAWEN AQUEDUCT is a more modest affair than Edstone, but it fights a running battle with juggernauts on the A34. On several occasions it has borne the brunt of high-sided vehicles whose drivers' sense of spacial awareness left something to be desired. Nevertheless, it has stood its ground since 1813 and should be good for a few years yet, especially as it has relatively recently been refurbished with the help of Heritage Lottery funding.

Wootton Wawen

Wootton Hall is a 17th century mansion which once belonged to Mrs Fitzherbert, a mistress of George IV. The parish church is of Saxon origin and considered one of Warwickshire's finest. A handsome former paper mill straddles the Alne.
THE NAVIGATION - canalside by the aqueduct. Tel: 01564 792676. Bar and restaurant meals. Nice garden.
HERON'S NEST - Coffee shop at Yew Tree Farm. Tel: 01564 792701. Also does B & B. General stores in the centre of the village and excellent farm shop selling fresh produce, home cooking and crafts.
TRAINS - hourly service to/from Birmingham and Stratford. Tel: 08457 484950.

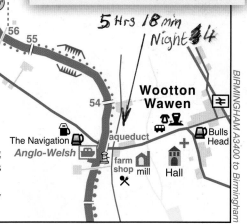

DELICATE split cantilever bridges and barrel-roofed cottages are two ingredients which lend particular charm to the middle section of the Stratford Canal. Actually, they only serve to 'gild the lily', because this length of canal is especially lovely in any case. Between Wootton Wawen and Kingswood the waterway loses itself in the last vestiges of the old Forest of Arden.

From Preston Bagot to Lowsonford the canal winds its lonely way across Yarningale Common, crossing Yarningale Aqueduct, the baby of the Stratford Canal family. The barrel-roofed cottages by locks 34 and 37 have been incorporated into modern extensions, but those by locks 28 and 31 remain unspoilt. The unusual design of these cottages is said to have been brought about by the use of the same wooden frames used in the construction of the brick road bridges which span the canal.

The abutments of a former railway bridge frame the canal near Lowsonford. The bridge carried a branchline to Henley-in-Arden, closed when the route was made obsolete by the opening of the North Warwickshire Railway. Legend has it that the track was despatched to The Front during the Great War but ended up at the bottom of the English Channel: *malheureusement,* it seems unlikely that the M40 will be as shortlived.

Woods border the canal, birdsong fills the air, the scent of wildflowers is intoxicating. Temple Thurston was equally taken with this part of the Stratford Canal. In 1910 he hired a narrowboat known as *The Flower of Gloster*, its captain Eynsham Harry, together with a horse called Fanny and set off on a journey of discovery which has remained a 'desert island' favourite of many canal enthusiasts ever since. Temple Thurston described the Stratford Canal as being 'right out of the track of the world'. He climbed the hillside to a farm at Yarningale for fresh milk, and Eynsham Harry bought beer from the wife of a lock-keeper. Reading *The Flower of Gloster* as you travel along the canal today leads inevitably to some melancholy comparisons.

Much improved of late, the towpath is mostly well-surfaced and wide and increasingly popular with ramblers - some nice interconnecting paths across Yarningale common as well.

The fact that this length of the canal is shopless but endowed with a pair of good pub/restaurants suggests that eating-out is a likely option: THE CRAB MILL at Preston Bagot (Tel: 01926 843342) is an attractive conversion of an old cider mill featuring comfortable leather sofas indoors and umbrellas out; excellent food and Wadworth and Belgian Leffe on tap. The FLEUR-DE-LYS at Lowsonford (Tel: 01564 782431) is a delightful country inn with a large canalside garden.

Lapworth Bottom Lock

11
26
39A
27
28
29
30
40
41
31
32
42
33
44
43
34
aqueduct
35
36
mp 16
45
46
37
38
47
48
60'
49
50
51
9

Fleur de Lys

Lowsonford

Nights Actual

mp 15

Preston Bagot
Crabmill
A4189
Preston Bagot Bottom Lock

Yarningale Common

Yarningale Aqueduct

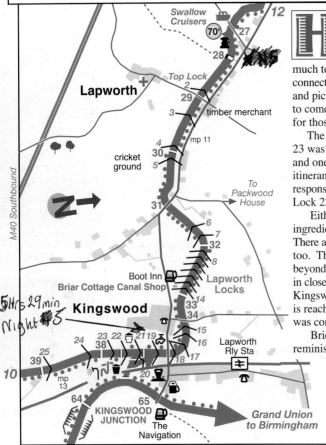

Lapworth

Swallow Cruisers

12

70'

27

28

Top Lock 2

29

timber merchant

3

4 mp 11

cricket ground

30

5

31

To Packwood House

6

7

32

8

Boot Inn

Lapworth Locks

Briar Cottage Canal Shop

Kingswood

33 14

34

15

16

Lapworth Rly Sta

18 17

24 23 22 21 19

38

25

39

20

10 mp 13

64 65

KINGSWOOD JUNCTION The Navigation

Grand Union to Birmingham

Grand Union to London

To Baddesley Clinton Hall

M40 Southbound

5Hrs 29 min Night 5

HOWEVER many times you've been there before, and whether you arrive by boat, by car or on foot, Kingswood Junction never fails to captivate. Either side of the junction the Stratford Canal continues with its unremitting locks, so boaters will be more than grateful to take a break here. Certainly there is much to see, and the configuration of the two briefly parallel canals, together with the connecting arm, allows plenty of opportunity for circular or figure-of-eight walks. A car park and picnic area, well masked by pine trees, encourage the non-boat-owning or hiring public to come to the junction, whilst the proximity of Lapworth railway station is advantageous for those environmentally-aware folk who favour the use of public transport.

The original connection between the Stratford and the Grand Union Canal below Lock 23 was reinstated in 1996, offering GU boaters bound for Stratford a saving of two locks, and one of the former reservoirs has been adapted for long term moorings. True to their itinerant ways, BW have vacated the former workshops by Lock 21, transferring day to day responsibility for the Stratford Canal all the way north to Fazeley. A new shower block above Lock 22 enables you to refresh those lock-stained bodies.

Either side of Kingswood there is much to look forward to encountering - all the tasty ingredients which create the Stratford Canal's unique flavour are encountered on this length. There are barrel-roofed cottages by Locks 21 and 25, and several of the charming split bridges too. The most dramatic section of the Lapworth flight lies between Bridges 32 and 33, beyond Kingswood Junction on the northern Stratford Canal. Here there are seven chambers in close proximity, presenting a spectacular view whether you are looking up or down. Leaving Kingswood bound for Kings Norton there are eighteen locks to negotiate before the summit is reached. The top lock is numbered '2' because the guillotine stop lock at Kings Norton was considered to be No 1.

Bridges 26 and 28 are lifting structures: the former of Llangollen pattern; the latter reminiscent of those found on the Oxford Canal. A winding hole by Bridge 27 marks the temporary terminus of the Stratford Canal between 1796 and 1800, a hiatus brought about by lack of capital. It actually took twenty-two years to build the twenty-five mile route between King's Norton and Stratford, which must be some sort of record.

The summit cost as much as the budget for the whole canal. The engineer was Josiah Clowes, who we will meet again in this guide on the Thames & Severn Canal.

Kingswood & Lapworth (Map 11)

Twin villages in North Warwickshire's commuter belt where the property prices routinely run into seven figures.

Eating & Drinking

THE NAVIGATION - canalside (Grand Union) Bridge 65. Unspoilt pub with lovely garden for hot days and cool interior for *really* hot days. Tel: 01564 783337.

THE BOOT - canalside Bridge 33. Well appointed country pub with sophisticated menu. Tel: 01564 782464.

Shopping

Village shop by railway bridge between the canals. Off licence by Bridge 65 (Grand Union). Gifts and canalia from the BRIAR COTTAGE canal shop by Bridge 33.

Things to Do

BADDESLEY CLINTON HALL AND PACKWOOD HOUSE - National Trust houses within walking distance of the canal. The former, a medieval manor house, lies one mile north-east of Bridge 65 (Grand Union), whilst the latter, a Tudor house, is one mile north of Bridge 31. Tel: 01564 783294 for details of both properties. TRAINS - local services to/from Leamington Spa, Warwick and Birmingham. Tel: 08457 484950.

Hockley Heath (Map 12)

From the road Hockley Heath looks like any other suburban settlement, the canal renders it more significant, if only for the facilities on offer and the chance of a well-earned break from travelling.

Eating & Drinking

HOCKLEY SPICE - Indian restaurant on A3400. Tel: 01564 784800.

Bridge 28

NAG'S HEAD - Harvester Restaurant. Tel: 01564 784137.

KAM SUNG - Chinese takeaway. Tel: 01564 782782.

WHARF TAVERN - canalside Bridge 25. Carvery meals and waterside garden overlooking stub of old wharf. Tel: 01564 782075.

Shopping

One-stop store, post office and Shell garage with shop (and cash machine) on one side of Bridge 25, newsagent and butcher on the other.

Connections

BUSES - service X20 usefully links Hockley Heath hourly Mon-Sat with Birmingham, Henley-in-Arden and Stratford-on-Avon. Tel: 0870 608 2 608.

Other Facilities on Map 12

At ILLSHAW HEATH, Wedge's marvellous bakery continues to flourish in its unlikely rural setting in the shadow of the M42. Fresh bread, sandwiches made to order, pies in profusion, mouthwatering cakes and puddings and a vegetable stall make it difficult for passing canaller's to resist.

Several excellent pubs are within easy reach of the canal. By Bridge 19, the BLUE BELL is a rare cider house, though naturally, in this day and age, beer and food are also available - Tel: 01564 702328. Near Bridge 17, the BULL'S HEAD on Lime Kiln Lane is a charming country pub with a good choice of food (Tel: 01564 702335) and you can say the same for the RED LION a quarter of a mile south of Bridge 16 (Tel: 01564 702325).

NORTH of Hockley Heath the canal assumes a mantle of trees which border the summit section. Oak, alder, hazel and willow predominate, creating a soothing, sylvan quality which, however beautiful, is apt to become soporific after a while. When you do catch glimpses of the surrounding countryside, it reminds you of the Home Counties, exuding an air of affluence epitomised by large detached houses, and horsey people, trotting down dappled lanes on dappled steeds.

The winding hole by Bridge 22 marks the site of a wharf once linked by tramway to the limestone quarries of Tanworth-in-Arden. Originally a branch canal had been planned to cater for this traffic. Near Bridge 19 an extensive miniature railway stands close to the canal, though hidden by a cutting. Privately owned, it does however, open to the public on selected dates.

At Earlswood an embankment carries the canal over Spring Brook and a feeder enters the canal from a trio of reservoirs which lie to the south-west. These Earlswood Reservoirs are a popular amenity, attracting ramblers, anglers and bird watchers.

Even if you have more enthusiasm for machinery than wildlife, the reservoirs are still worth visiting to see the old engine house on Lady Lane, to which narrowboats carried coal up the feeder until 1936. Earlswood Motor Yacht Club members use the feeder now for moorings.

Like a dart player's waistline, Birmingham's southern suburbs keep on expanding and new housing borders the canal at Dickens Heath. Significantly architects are now keen to incorporate canals into their vision, whereas a generation ago ugly boundary fences would have been erected and the houses would have turned their backs to the water. One of the new developments even incorporates a prodigious canalside waterfall and it looks as though bars and shops may well ensue.

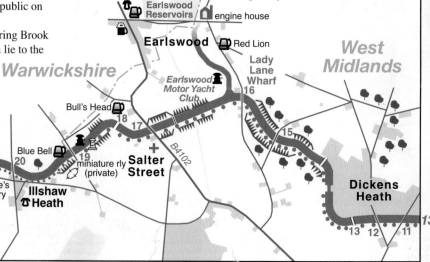

For details of facilities see page 29

ALTHOUGH the map emphasises how built-up these south-western suburbs of Birmingham are, the canal seems oblivious to the proximity of so many houses and people, retaining an aloof quality, like a recluse in a crowd. The boater's steady progress is interrupted by having to throttle down past moored boats at the bottom of gardens. Another obstacle to progress is Shirley Drawbridge, not so much a local-lass, more a wind-lass operated lift bridge on a busyish by-road, necessitating the use of barriers accessed with a British Waterways' Yale key. Perhaps Shirley is a staunch supporter of Wake Green Amateurs, a football club whose ground abuts the lift bridge. South of Bridge 5 are the impressive premises of Yardley Wood Bus Garage.

Shakespeare looks inscrutably down from the western portal of Brandwood Tunnel. Brandwood was built without a towpath, so horses were led over the top while boats were worked through by the simple expedient of boatmen pulling on a handrail set into the tunnel lining. The horse path still provides walkers with a right of way and also offers access to some useful suburban shops.

Between the tunnel and King's Norton Junction stands a disused swing bridge with a history, a *cause celebre* in the embryonic days of the Inland Waterways Association. It was originally a lift bridge and, during the Second World War the Great Western Railway, who owned the canal at that time, clamped down the platform following damage by a lorry. Commercial traffic had ceased on the canal, but the IWA maintained that a right of navigation still applied. The GWR claimed that they would be only too happy to jack up the bridge to permit boats to pass as required, little realising that the IWA intended to organise as many boat passages as would be necessary to have the bridge fully repaired. Several campaign cruises ensued, but it was not until Nationalisation that the present swing bridge was installed. Often erroneously referred to as Lifford Lane Bridge, Bridge 2 is in fact on Tunnel Lane.

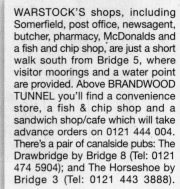

WARSTOCK'S shops, including Somerfield, post office, newsagent, butcher, pharmacy, McDonalds and a fish and chip shop, are just a short walk south from Bridge 5, where visitor moorings and a water point are provided. Above BRANDWOOD TUNNEL you'll find a convenience store, a fish & chip shop and a sandwich shop/cafe which will take advance orders on 0121 444 004. There's a pair of canalside pubs: The Drawbridge by Bridge 8 (Tel: 0121 474 5904); and The Horseshoe by Bridge 3 (Tel: 0121 443 3888).

Worcester & Birmingham

Wast Hill Tunnel,
King's Norton

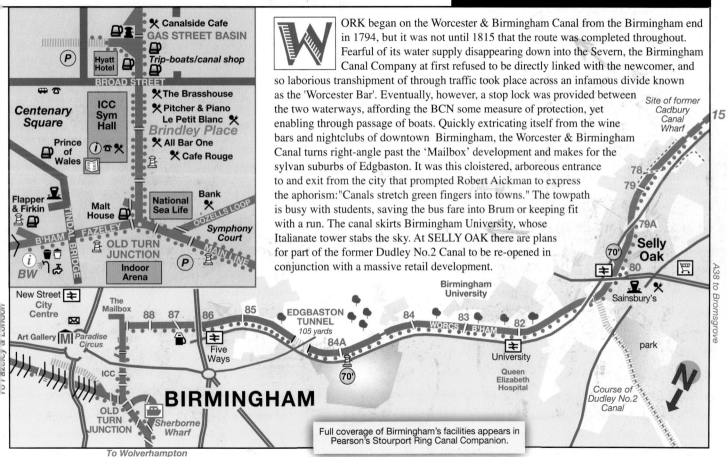

WORK began on the Worcester & Birmingham Canal from the Birmingham end in 1794, but it was not until 1815 that the route was completed throughout. Fearful of its water supply disappearing down into the Severn, the Birmingham Canal Company at first refused to be directly linked with the newcomer, and so laborious transhipment of through traffic took place across an infamous divide known as the 'Worcester Bar'. Eventually, however, a stop lock was provided between the two waterways, affording the BCN some measure of protection, yet enabling through passage of boats. Quickly extricating itself from the wine bars and nightclubs of downtown Birmingham, the Worcester & Birmingham Canal turns right-angle past the 'Mailbox' development and makes for the sylvan suburbs of Edgbaston. It was this cloistered, arboreous entrance to and exit from the city that prompted Robert Aickman to express the aphorism:"Canals stretch green fingers into towns." The towpath is busy with students, saving the bus fare into Brum or keeping fit with a run. The canal skirts Birmingham University, whose Italianate tower stabs the sky. At SELLY OAK there are plans for part of the former Dudley No.2 Canal to be re-opened in conjunction with a massive retail development.

Full coverage of Birmingham's facilities appears in Pearson's Stourport Ring Canal Companion.

33

VON RING travellers pass from the Stratford to the Worcester & Birmingham at King's Norton. The old guillotine stop lock which once jealously guarded waters of the two canals is still intact, and though long disused, a fine and photogenic survival. A sizeable paper mill formerly overlooked the canal junction and large quantities of coal were brought here by narrowboat from Black Country mines for many years. Nail-making was another facet of the local economy which brought trade to the canal.

Canal trade was even more brisk to and from Cadbury's famous chocolate factory at Bournville. Commercial activity on the canal is sadly no longer considered a viable proposition, but leisure boating does bring its fair share of visitors to Cadbury World (see page 38) notwithstanding the slightly intimidating nature of the security fenced moorings provided alongside Bournville railway station and an accompanying recommendation that you leave no valuables on board because 'thieves operate in the area'!

Bournville's garden village owes its existence to the altruism of Quakers Richard and George Cadbury, who built a chocolate factory on a greenfield site in the vicinity in 1879. It was George in particular who had vision's of a worker's paradise, commissioning the architect Alexander Harvey to design artisans dwellings on a 120 acre site. Each house was to have a garden with fruit trees and a vegetable patch to provide an element of self-sufficiency - one cannot live on chocolate alone. Between bridges 75 and 73 the towpath swaps sides, not on a whim, but because the Midland Railway once operated a transhipment basin on the west bank of the canal.

At 2,726 yards, WAST HILL TUNNEL is the Worcester & Birmingham's longest. It takes around half an hour to pass through and, whilst appearances can be deceptive, rest assured that there *is* room to pass oncoming craft inside its gloomy depths. Like all Worcester & Birmingham tunnels (except Edgbaston), it has no towpath. The lads

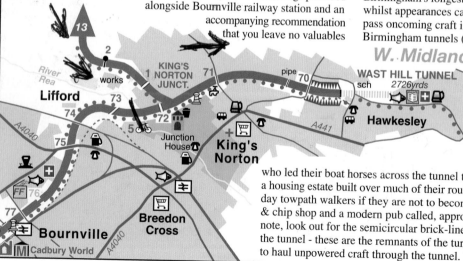

who led their boat horses across the tunnel top in the past would be flummoxed now to find a housing estate built over much of their route, and a degree of diligence is required of latter-day towpath walkers if they are not to become lost. Consolation comes in the guise of a fish & chip shop and a modern pub called, appropriately enough, 'The Tunnel'! On an historic note, look out for the semicircular brick-lined embrasures in the canal bank at either end of the tunnel - these are the remnants of the turning points for tugs which were once employed to haul unpowered craft through the tunnel.

For details of facilities at Bournville and King's Norton see page 38

POST-WAR Alvechurch overspills up its hillside to impinge upon the canal, but barely deflects from its dreamy, lockless progress above the valley of the River Arrow. There are panoramic views eastwards towards Weatheroak Hill crossed by the Roman's Ryknild Street. A feeder comes in from Upper Bittell Reservoir beside an isolated canal employee's cottage near Bridge 66. The Lower Reservoir, rich in wildfowl, lies alongside the canal and is given a gorgeous wooded backdrop by the Lickey Hills. Only the Upper Reservoir feeds the canal, the Lower was provided to compensate millers whose water supplies from the Arrow had been detrimentally affected by construction of the canal. A short section of the canal was re-routed in 1985 to accommodate construction of the M42 motorway. Alvechurch FC of the Midland Alliance can lay claim to the lengthiest FA Cup tie of all time. In 1971 it took five replays and an

incredible eleven hours of play before the fourth round qualifying tie against Oxford City was decided in 'The Church's' favour. Sadly, after all that effort, they were knocked out in the first round proper!

Bridge 62 carries the electrified Redditch-Birmingham commuter line across the canal, Avon Ringer's will recall seeing the route, which originally continued to Ashchurch on the outskirts of Tewkesbury, abandoned at Evesham (Map 4). The approach cuttings to Shortwood Tunnel can be so suffocated by the odour of wild garlic that you feel as if you are being embraced by an over enthusiastic Frenchman. All that's missing is the tang of Gauloise, but then you may be able to provide that yourself. The old horse-path across the top remains well-defined, and it is pleasant to wander across the top, fantasising that you've a horse to lead while your boat is hauled through the earth beneath your feet by one of the erstwhile tunnel tugs, as described so evocatively by Tom Foxon in his regrettably long out of print book *Number One*.

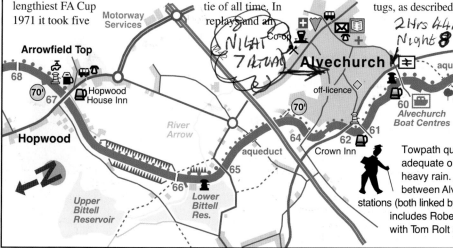

Towpath quality varies between good and adequate on this section; it can be muddy after heavy rain. A popular five mile walk is that between Alvechurch and Bromsgrove railway stations (both linked by regular trains to/from Birmingham) which includes Robert Aickman's route to his historic meeting with Tom Rolt at Tardebigge in 1945 (see Map 17).

B4120 to Barnt Green   BIRMINGHAM

For details of facilities at Hopwood and Alvechurch see page 38

TARDEBIGGE represents a boater's Rite of Passage. Once you have tackled this flight which, coupled with the neighbouring six at Stoke, amount to thirty-six locks in four miles, other groups of locks, however fiendish, however formidable, pale into insignificance. The thirty chambers of the Tardebigge flight raise the canal over two hundred feet, the top lock - somewhat removed from the rest - being, at 14 feet, one of the deepest narrowbeam locks on the system; it replaced a lift prone to malfunction and water wastage. Well maintained and surrounded by fine countryside, with wonderful views to the Malvern Hills, Tardebigge Locks are there to be enjoyed, not dreaded. And in the summer months you'll have plenty of fellow travellers with whom to share the experience, not to mention the work! Tardebigge's 18th century church, with its slender 135ft spire, is an inspirational landmark: 'belatedly baroque' in the words of James Lees-Milne in his pithy 1964 *Shell Guide to Worcestershire*.

Tardebigge holds a special place in the story of the inland waterways movement. It was to here that Robert Aickman and his wife made their way from Bromsgrove railway station to meet Tom and Angela Rolt aboard their narrowboat home *Cressy* which had been moored above the top lock throughout the Second World War. As a direct result of their meeting the Inland Waterways Association was formed. A plinth adjacent to the lock tells the story, along with a supplementary plaque correcting the date to 1945 - as Pearsons had maintained all along!

Only the briefest of pounds separates the Tardebigge and Stoke flights. Room enough, just, for half a dozen boats to moor for an overnight breather. The picturesque lock-keeper's cottage between locks 31 and 32 is available for holiday lets from the admirable Landmark Trust (Tel: 01628 825925) a body devoted to the rescue and refurbishment of worthwhile buildings in all shapes and sizes. It was the demolition of the junction house at Hurleston, on the Shropshire Union Canal, which 'maddened' the Trust's founder, John Smith, into creating the organisation in 1965.

For details of facilities at Aston Fields and Stoke Wharf see page 38

Early morning patrol, Lock 50, Tardebigge

Bournville (Map 15)

Use of a BW Yale key provides access from the secure offside moorings opposite Bournville railway station to suburban shops and take-aways and CADBURY WORLD, whose opening times etc can be obtained by telephoning 0121 451 4180.

King's Norton (Map 15)

KING'S NORTON provides the most easily accessible facilities for canal travellers in this area. 48 hour moorings are provided between bridges 71 and 72 and it's only a short uphill walk to the centre of this busy suburban settlement grouped about a pretty green and overlooked by the imposing spire of St Nicholas' Church. Facilities include: a pharmacy, Spar shop, newsagent, off licence, post office and Lloyds TSB bank with cash machines. There's an Indian restaurant and takeaway and two pubs.

Hopwood (Map 16)

The HOPWOOD HOUSE INN (Tel: 0121 445 1716) is a large, refurbished roadhouse alongside Bridge 67. There's a garage with shop across the road.

Alvechurch (Map 16)

It's one thing strolling down from the canal, but an altogether different matter struggling back with shopping bags. Nevertheless, Alvechurch is a pleasant village with some worthwhile facilities, though if you are not up to the trek a modest range of provisions is obtainable at the boatyard shop in addition to a good choice of canalia.

Eating & Drinking

THE WEIGHBRIDGE - canalside Bridge 60. Tel: 0121 445 5511. Part of Alvechurch Boat Centres boatyard, and the 'weighbridge house' for a coal wharf in days gone by. Tillerman's Tipple is brewed for them by Weatheroak. Home cooked food lunchtimes and evenings; breakfasts by prior arrangement.

THE CROWN - canalside Bridge 61. Tel: 0121 445 2300. An unspoilt canalside pub.

Shopping

Alvechurch lies twenty minutes walk down from the canal but boasts a useful range of shops: Co-op, post office (with newspapers) pharmacy, butcher, off licence, and bakery, but no bank. There is also a Chinese (Tel: 0121 447 8085) takeaway and an Indian restaurant (Tel: 0121 445 5660). Real ale enthusiasts may like to seek out Weatheroak Ales off licence just down the road from Bridge 61 - Tel: 0121 445 4411.

Connections

TRAINS - half-hourly service to Redditch and Birmingham (Tel: 08457 484950).

Aston Fields (Map 17)

Aston Fields, a suburb of Bromsgrove, has a number of useful shops - notably BANNERS deli and hot food outlet established as long ago as 1906 (Tel: 01527 872581) as well as the town's railway station. For Taxis contact 'Bill's of Bromsgrove on 01527 832594

Stoke Wharf (Map 17)

Canalside pubs include the QUEEN'S HEAD by Bridge 48 (Tel: 01527 877777) and the NAVIGATION by Bridge 44 (Tel: 01527 870194). AVONCROFT MUSEUM, a mile north of Bridge 48, houses a wonderful collection of buildings saved from demolition (Tel: 01527 831363). The LITTLE SHOP by Bridge 44 (Tel: 01527 876438) deals in Calor Gas, coal and chandlery.

Stoke Works (Map 18)

The BOAT & RAILWAY (Tel: 01527 831065) is a Banks's pub with a nice canalside terrace, good choice of beers and a wide range of bar meals (not Sundays) and a skittle alley. The Worcester & Birmingham Canal Society regularly meet here. There's a butcher and a post office stores on a housing estate half a mile north of Bridge 42.

Hanbury Wharf (Map 18)

At Hanbury Wharf the EAGLE & SUN (Tel: 01905 770130) is perennially popular with boaters, perhaps on account of the generously-sized bar meals that are served. Shops are conspicuous by their absence hereabouts, although a range of basic provisions is available from the boatyard along with guides, maps and postcards.

Dunhampstead (Map 19)

The quiet hamlet of Dunhampstead is able to offer both a canalside craft shop and a well-appointed pub called THE FIR TREE INN (Tel: 01905 774094) which serves tasty food and Hook Norton within its designer interior, and you can also learn about the dastardly Oddingley Murders.

Tibberton (Map 19)

Tibberton's amenities include a post office stores which also sells newspapers (lunchtime closing and early closing Wed, Sat & Sun) and two Bank's pubs, the BRIDGE INN (Tel: 01905 345684) is the more canal orientated, having a large waterside garden and offering a good choice of food; however the SPEED THE PLOUGH (Tel: 01905 345602) can also be recommended. Buses connect the village with Worcester - Tel: 0870 608 2 608.

NOWADAYS, Britain's salt industry is largely confined to Cheshire but, as the name Droitwich suggests, this part of Worcestershire was once a centre of salt making too. The salt obsessed Romans built a special road between Droitwich and Alcester to carry this valuable commodity. Similarly, the Worcester & Birmingham built the short Droitwich Junction Canal from Hanbury Wharf to carry the same cargo. Barely two miles long, it included seven locks and passed briefly into the River Salwarpe before meeting the previously established Droitwich Canal at Vines Park near the town centre. Both the Droitwich canals had lapsed into dereliction before the end of the Thirties. In recent years they have undergone varying degrees of restoration: at Hanbury Wharf the first three locks have been restored and the top pound of the Junction Canal has been re-watered and is in use as private moorings. The summit of the widebeam Droitwich Canal is also in water and a day boat is available for hire from the Droitwich Canal Company - see page 94. Full restoration is earmarked for 2007.

At the end of the 18th century, John Corbett, son of a local boatman, discovered large deposits of brine at Stoke Prior and developed one of the largest saltworks in the world on the site. It made his fortune. He met an Irish woman in Paris, married her and built a replica French chateau for her on the outskirts of Droitwich, a town he transformed from one of industrial squalor into a fashionable spa. In its heyday the canalside works at Stoke was producing 200,000 tons of salt a year. The company had a fleet of narrowboats and hundreds of railway wagons. Corbett died in 1901 and is buried at the pretty little church of St Michael's, Stoke Prior (Map 17). His vast works, later part of ICI, was demolished in the 1970s.

Attractive countryside returns at ASTWOOD LOCKS, as canal and railway drift lazily through lush farmland overlooked by the wooded slopes of Summer Hill to the east. Westward views encompass Abberley and Woodbury hills beyond the River Severn. Closer at hand are the twin 700ft high masts of Wychbold radio transmitting station. Opened in 1934, its call sign "Droitwich Calling" became known throughout Britain and in many parts of Europe. During the Second World War Droitwich's long range transmitter broadcast the 'voice of freedom' throughout occupied Europe.

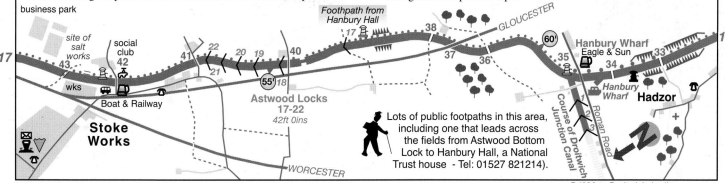

For details of facilities at Stoke Works and Hanbury Wharf see opposite

HE canal skirts the mellow settlements of Shernal Green, Dunhampstead, Oddingley and Tibberton and, in spite of being sandwiched by the railway and motorway, seems remote and untouched. High clumps of sedge border the canal, swaying with the passage of boats and somehow emphasising the loneliness of the landscape. At Shernal Green the Wychavon Way - a 42-mile long distance footpath running from Holt Fleet on the River Severn to Winchcombe in Gloucesterhire - makes its way over the canal. 'Severn & Avon Ring' boaters will encounter the path again at Cropthorne where it crosses the River Avon by way of Jubilee Bridge.

DUNHAMPSTEAD TUNNEL is tiny compared to the 'big three' to the north, but like them it has no towpath, forcing walkers to take to the old horse-path through deciduous woodlands above. A hire base adds traffic to the canal at this point, whilst a craft shop and convivial country pub provide an excuse to break your journey.

ODDINGLEY consists of little more than an ancient manor house, a tiny church and a level-crossing keeper's cabin of typical Midland Railway style. Murder was done here in 1806!

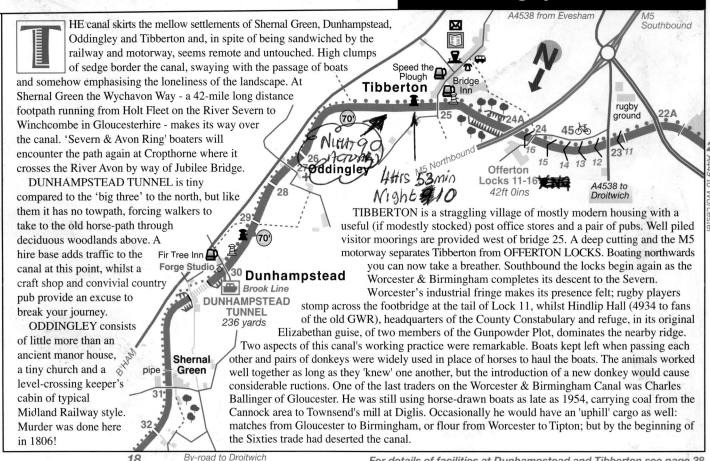

TIBBERTON is a straggling village of mostly modern housing with a useful (if modestly stocked) post office stores and a pair of pubs. Well piled visitor moorings are provided west of bridge 25. A deep cutting and the M5 motorway separates Tibberton from OFFERTON LOCKS. Boating northwards you can now take a breather. Southbound the locks begin again as the Worcester & Birmingham completes its descent to the Severn.

Worcester's industrial fringe makes its presence felt; rugby players stomp across the footbridge at the tail of Lock 11, whilst Hindlip Hall (4934 to fans of the old GWR), headquarters of the County Constabulary and refuge, in its original Elizabethan guise, of two members of the Gunpowder Plot, dominates the nearby ridge. Two aspects of this canal's working practice were remarkable. Boats kept left when passing each other and pairs of donkeys were widely used in place of horses to haul the boats. The animals worked well together as long as they 'knew' one another, but the introduction of a new donkey would cause considerable ructions. One of the last traders on the Worcester & Birmingham Canal was Charles Ballinger of Gloucester. He was still using horse-drawn boats as late as 1954, carrying coal from the Cannock area to Townsend's mill at Diglis. Occasionally he would have an 'uphill' cargo as well: matches from Gloucester to Birmingham, or flour from Worcester to Tipton; but by the beginning of the Sixties trade had deserted the canal.

For details of facilities at Dunhampstead and Tibberton see page 38

ATERSIDE Worcester has always enjoyed a flagrant love affair with the Severn, but in recent times the canal has come into its own. From Tolladine down, the towpath is designated a 'pedway' and popular with pedestrians and cyclists alike. Burgeoning industrial estates accompany the canal but do little to spoil it. Cadbury's once had a busy wharf at Blackpole linked by water transport to their premises at Bournville (Map 15) and Frampton-on-Severn (Map 28). A leisure centre and municipal golf course border the canal above Bilford Upper Lock. Worcester City, a non league football club, have a substantial ground, signposted by tall floodlights, beside Bridge 12. North of Bridge 11 school playing fields are overlooked by an imposing pavilion.

A shapely railway bridge spans the canal by Lowesmoor Wharf. It has a hole cut out of it, presumably to lessen the weight of the structure. Lowesmoor Wharf is a good spot to moor securely (Mon-Wed only) close to the city centre - just slip beneath the roving bridge and ask permission at the boatyard office.

An Italianate clock tower peeps over the canal by Bridge 8, the former Engine Works of 1864. In contrast new retail units have been

Map labels

A449 from M5

DROITWICH

Tolladine Lock 7ft 0ins
industrial estate

Black Pole Lock 7ft 0ins

rems of Cadbury wharf

golf course

Leisure Centre

Gregory's Mill Locks 14ft 0ins

Bilford Locks 14ft 0ins

Worcester City F.C.

WORCESTER

Rowing !

Race Course

Shrub Hill

Blockhouse Lock 11ft 0ins

Sidbury Lock 11ft 0ins

Foregate St.

City Centre

Cathedral

Worcester Bridge

McDonalds

cricket ground

ferry

Diglis Canal Locks 18ft 0ins

Diglis River Locks 7ft 11ins
Tel: 01905 354280

Weir !

LOWESMOOR 70'

Viking

Fort Royal Park

Commandery

Fownes Hotel

Cinema   City

London Road

Royal Worcs

Centre

Diglis Basins
Tel: 01905 358758

basin   basin

lock-keeper

drydock

RIVER SEVERN →

pontoon

(handwritten notes) COMMANDERY B BOATS · O'NITE NIGHT OPTION · 5Hrs 38min Night t0 11

R. Severn to Stourport

provided with a linking footbridge numbered 5A. Fownes Hotel was once a glove factory. Almost opposite stands The Commandery. Charles II used this building as his headquarters during the Civil War Battle of Worcester in 1651, though it was originally a hospital and dates from as early as the 15th century. There is space here for some half a dozen boats to moor overnight within mellifluous earshot of the cathedral clock. Sidbury Lock lies near the site of a gate in the city wall where a thousand Royalist troops are said to have been killed. Cromwell's men had captured the nearby fort and turned its canons on the escaping Cavaliers. The elevated fort is a pleasant park now, easily reached from the Commandery moorings. A panoramic plaque identifies major incidents of the Battle of Worcester and the gardens offer a marvellous view over the city.

Industry reasserts itself as the canal passes the famous Royal Worcester porcelain works and Townsend's Mill. The latter, refurbished for accommodation, was once an intensive user of water transport, via both canal and river, but nowadays the only traffic hereabouts is of the pleasure variety, all regular trade on this waterway having ceased by the Sixties.

DIGLIS BASINS opened in the 19th century to facilitate transhipment of cargoes between river and canal. Redevelopment has largely eroded the latent atmosphere of this inland port, but it would be carping to criticise British Waterways too much for cashing in on the inherent value of such sites - they need all the income they can muster to keep the canals ticking over. Two broad locks separate the basins from the river. They are closed overnight, re-opening about eight in the morning when the lock-keeper comes on duty. Mostly he doesn't get involved in operating them, but it's good to know he's about should you require his help or advice. Entering or leaving the river can pose problems, especially if the current is flowing quickly, and getting your crew on or off for the locks needs careful consideration. One of the easiest access points is the pontoon immediately downstream of the lock entrance. Downstream there is a third Diglis Lock, in fact an automated pair, that on the east bank being the smaller of the two.

Lowesmoor, Worcester

Worcester *(Map 20)*

Descending from Birmingham to Worcester, the West Midlands are left intuitively behind, and you find yourself in streets where the patois has a distinct West Country burr. 'Royal' Worcester suffered more than most at the hands of the developers during the Sixties (Ian Nairn, the late architectural writer and broadcaster, was incensed, and James Lees-Milne got into hot water for permitting his *Shell Guide to Worcestershire* to be too critical) but much making of amends has been done in recent years to enhance the city's fabric. The Cathedral, gazing devoutly over the Severn, belongs - along with Gloucester and Hereford - to a golden triangle of ecclesiastical paragons which share Europe's oldest music festival, 'The Three Choirs'. From the deep well of Worcester's history you can draw inspiration from almost any era that captures your imagination. This was the 'faithful city' of the Civil War from which Charles II escaped following the final defeat of the Cavaliers. It was the home, for much of his life, of Sir Edward Elgar. Home too of the manufacturers of Royal Worcester porcelain and that ensign of the empire, Lea & Perrins sauce. And here you'll find one of the country's loveliest cricketing venues, Worcestershire's New Road ground - Tel: 01905 748474. So in any boating itinerary, Worcester deserves to be allotted at least half a day in your schedule.

Eating & Drinking

BROWNS RESTAURANT - Quay Street. Tel: 01905 26263. Worth blowing the budget here for the ambience of this former riverside mill, let alone quality of the cooking.

BENEDICTO'S - Sidbury. Tel: 01905 21444. Italian on the Cathedral side of Sidbury Lock.

HODSON - High Street. Tel: 01905 21036. Long established cafe restaurant near the Cathedral and

Diglis

Elgar's statue. Ideal for morning coffee.

DIGLIS HOUSE HOTEL - Riverside. Tel: 01905 353518. Best to moor in basins and walk back for good bar and restaurant meals; nice views over the Severn.

SALMON'S LEAP - Severn Street. Quiet real ale pub within easy reach of Diglis. Tel: 01905 726260.

THE ANCHOR - Diglis Basin. Tel: 01905 351094. Down to earth Banks's boozer for prodigious Swallowers and Amazons; lunches and takeaway baguettes from 9am: a last redoubt of the old Diglis!

Shopping

Worcester is an excellent city in which to shop. Two refurbished shopping areas are The Hopmarket and Crown Passage. The Shambles, Friar Street and New Street feature numerous fascinating little shops and small businesses. Crown Gate is the main shopping precinct with adjoining street markets on Tue, Wed, Fri & Sat. If you are making the *faux pas* of boating through non-stop, then a butcher and pharmacy stand within seconds of Sidbury Lock.

Things to Do

TOURIST INFORMATION CENTRE - The Guildhall, High Street. Tel: 01905 726311. Worcester appears to have more visitor centres than any other provincial city of its size. A thorough list defies our space limitations, but obvious highlights are: THE COMMANDERY (canalside by Sidbury Lock - Tel: 01905 361821) which was Charles II's headquarters during the Civil War; ROYAL WORCESTER (Severn Street, near Sidbury Lock again - Tel: 01905 746000), the porcelain and bone china makers; THE GUILDHALL (High Street - Tel: 01905 723471); and THE CATHEDRAL (Tel: 01905 611002, dating from the 11th century and the burial place of King John.

Connections

TRAINS - stations at Foregate Street and Shrub Hill. Services to/from the Malverns (nice idea for an excursion), Droitwich, Kidderminster, Birmingham etc. Tel: 08457 484950.

BUSES - Tel: 0870 608 2 608.

TAXIS - Cathedral Cars. Tel: 01905 767400.

The River Severn

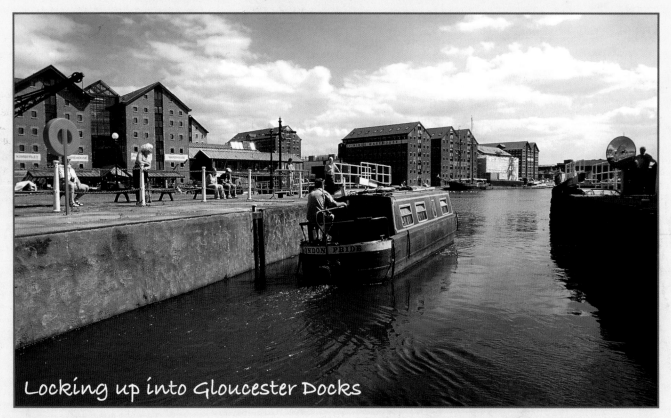

Locking up into Gloucester Docks

IKE a deferential waitress coming to clear the dishes, the River Teme makes little impact on the haughty Severn, but on its way down from the Welsh Marches, past Ludlow and through lush Herefordshire pastures, this lovely river hits heights of beauty that the Severn never attains.

William Sandys, who was originally responsible for making the River Avon navigable, acquired the rights to make the Teme navigable up to Ludlow in the 17th century, but he never got around to doing anything about it. Perhaps the Civil War impeded his plans. Just a canon ball's trajectory from here the first skirmish of that conflict took place at Powick Bridge on September 23rd 1642. The Parliamentarians lost that battle but came from behind to win the war by defeating the Royalist forces on virtually the same battlefield nine years later. A long abandoned jetty hints at the former trade in oil and petroleum along the river. The long established Severn Motor Yacht Club own a nice weatherboarded clubhouse beside their private moorings just downstream of the Worcester by-pass crossing.

South of Worcester the Severn pursues an undemonstrative course. There are brief glimpses of the Malvern Hills beyond the river's high, and largely uninspiring, banks. But if the scenery momentarily falters, the novelty of deep, wide water has yet to wear off.

KEMPSEY comes bravely down to the riverbank but the passing boater sees little more than a long line of pontoon moorings belonging to the Seaborne Yacht Company boatyard. The A38 trunk road bisects the village and much modern housing has engulfed the core of the original settlement.

An old ferry house marks the site of a former river crossing at PIXHAM. In his informative account of fords and ferries on the Severn in Worcestershire (published locally in 1982), H. W. Gwilliam relates that the ferry here was capable of carrying motor vehicles until it ceased operating around the time of the Second World War. It seems that there was no formal road approach to the ferry stage on the Kempsey side, so cars had to be driven across the field as best they could. The local hunt used the ferry too and it must have been some sight to see the hounds packed aboard the vessel - except for the unfortunate fox, of course. In the absence of the ferry the Severn Way is forced to detour inland.

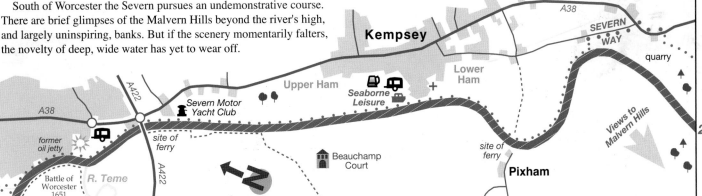

UNDER the watchful eye of the Malverns, the River Severn winds past occasional outcrops of sandstone rock - welcome interludes of drama amid the monotony of the willow-lined banks: the boater can only envy walkers on the Severn Way whose views are far more encompassing. From the old wharf at Severn Stoke, for example, you can see the Panorama Tower at Croome D'Abitot to the east, a folly in landscaped grounds which were the work of Capability Brown.

Nevertheless, this is probably the prettiest part of the river between Worcester and Tewkesbury, and though there are few formal moorings, owners of shallow-draughted cruisers seem prepared to tie up to overhanging tree trunks and enjoy a peaceful picnic. Clevelode is a pleasant little community of orchards and cottages but just

downstream lies one of those caravan parks that the Severn seems fated to attract. There were ferries both here and at RHYDD. The sandstone outcrop extended across the bed of the river and caused problems with navigation before the locks were built.

If the rocky bluffs have a Rhineland quality about them, then, in the context of the Severn Plain, the Malverns are positively Alpine. They represent the highest point along Latitude 52 between the Black Mountains of Wales and the Harz Mountains in Germany. It is impossible not to be moved by their brooding presence. They were the inspiration behind much of Sir Edward Elgar's music, though the Severn also played a part in exciting his muse. 'I am still at heart the dreamy child who used to be found in the reeds by Severn side with a sheet of paper, trying to fix the sounds and longing for something great'.

An ostentatious, castellated mansion towers above the woods at Severn Bank and an old boathouse stands on the river below Severn End, but barely any trace survives of the former quay at Hanley Castle. In bygone days isolated villages like these would have relied on the river for transport.

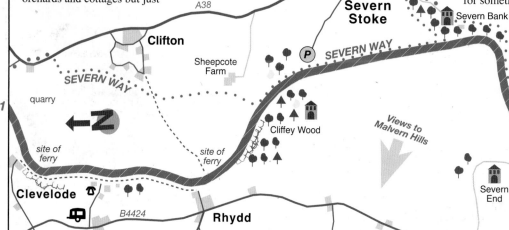

UPTON-ON-SEVERN'S fleshpots come as welcome relief to the Severn's somewhat repetitive scenery. Two road bridges span this section of the Severn. The present bridge at UPTON dates from the Second World War. It replaced a swing bridge, the abutments of which can still be seen. Each plod along the road of Progress apparently rids us of something worthwhile: fords give way to ferries, ferries to swing bridges, swing bridges to fixed structures devoid of any character. And now we can travel so quickly that the average journey makes no impression on us whatsoever, all of which succinctly explains the appeal of inland waterway travel. The railway bridge which carried the Malvern and Tewkesbury line over the Severn would have been well worth seeing too, as it originally was equipped with a sliding central section which could be moved aside to permit tall-masted vessels to pass. Look out for the new aggregate wharves which have brought welcome barge traffic back to the river.

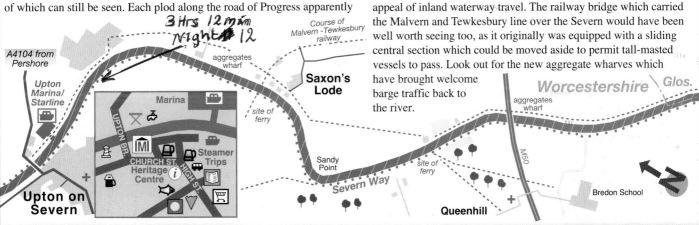

Upton-on-Severn

The spirit of the Severn pervades this charming little town, lending it the atmosphere of a small coastal port, an illusion enhanced by the resemblance of the cupola-topped old church to a lighthouse. Upton shares with Brecon the distinction of being both on the inland waterway network and hosting a jazz festival, in this instance, on the last weekend in June. Limited visitor pontoon moorings are provided upstream of the bridge.

Eating & Drinking

WHITE LION HOTEL - High Street. Comfortable hotel (mentioned in *Tom Jones* by Henry Fielding) with popular Brasserie. Tel: 01684 592551.
PUNDITS - Old Street. Cosy Bangladeshi restaurant and takeaway. Tel: 01684 591022.

Shopping

Shopping as it should be in a number of highly individual shops, good delicatessens, bakers, butchers and greengrocers; Lloyds TSB and HSBC banks. Interesting specialist map shop, old-fashioned sweet shop, and secondhand bookshop. Small SPAR and CO-OP supermarkets and launderette.

Things to Do

TOURIST INFORMATION - High Street. Tel: 01684 594200.
UPTON HERITAGE CENTRE - Church Street. Small museum tracing Upton's history. Tel: 01684 592679.

Connections

BUSES - Services to/from Worcester and Tewkesbury. Tel: 0870 608 2 608.

former station
(closed 1961)

Tewkesbury

Deerhurst

Odda's Chapel
Sailing !

1Hr 46min
Night3

Town Centre

Abbey

Lower Lode
Cheltenham College
Boat House

SEVERN WAY

25

*Tewkesbury
Marina*

WC

P

flour mill

ferry

Old
Ferry
Inn

sailing
club

**Chaceley
Stock**

1

**Avon
Lock**

*Severn
Ham*

water
works

*Lower
Lode*

*By-road to
Forthampton*

*By-road to
Chaceley*

Weir !

The Mythe

Mythe Bridge

N11

**Upper Lode
Lock**

A38 from Worcester

SEVERN WAY

course of Midland Railway
Ashchurch - Malvern line

Bushley

Summary of Facilities

Two excellent riverside pubs provide the refreshment opportunities along this length of the Severn. The LOWER LODE INN (Tel: 01684 293224), with BW moorings close by, does food, accommodation, and - not least of all - Donnington BB bitter from Stow in the Wold. The OLD FERRY INN at Chaceley Stock (Tel: 01452 780333) is a former cider making house offering bar and restaurant meals in a pleasant setting.

N contrast to the aesthetic shortcomings of the two bridges upstream, MYTHE BRIDGE is handsome in the extreme, a single iron span dating from 1825. You only have to see it to guess that it is the work of that Botticelli of bridge builders, Thomas Telford. This is one of half a dozen bridges that Telford built across the Severn; its setting, below the wooded heights of Mythe Cliff, is sublime.

The confluence with the navigable channel of the Avon soon follows, but if you're bound for Gloucester or Sharpness you proceed to UPPER LODE LOCK, which was built in 1858 to alleviate the problem of shallows experienced upstream, particularly in the vicinity of Upton. Likely as not, the lock-keeper will lower you a bucket; not, disappointingly, full of freshly caught elvers, but containing a useful instruction sheet pertaining to the passage downstream to Gloucester. A second channel of the Avon enters the Severn at LOWER LODE, from where the view of Tewkesbury Abbey, with Bredon Hill as a backdrop, is quite breathtaking. A passenger ferry operates here in the summer months and is popular with walkers, cyclists and patrons of the Lower Lode Hotel. How sad it is that access to Deerhurst and its Saxon church is denied the boater; it's hard to imagine the cost of a mooring pontoon would prove excessive.

Glos.

Worcs.

N

23

For Tewkesbury detail see Map 1

Poppies at Upper Lode

Apperley (Map 25)

Once a village known for apple growing and salmon fishing, Apperley now exists chiefly as a commuter base for folk who work in Gloucester and Cheltenham and there is no longer enough daytime activity to support a shop.

THE COAL HOUSE - riverside with pontoon moorings.Tel: 01452 780211.

Haw Bridge (Map 25)

A British Waterways mooring pontoon and two good inns make this a popular staging post for boaters.

Eating & Drinking

THE RIVERSIDE INN - riverside to north of bridge. Tel: 01452 780275. Charmingly old fashioned and well regarded for its steaks and grills; nice garden to rear.

HAW BRIDGE INN - riverside to south of bridge. Tel: 01452 780316. A convivial Wadworth pub.

RED LION - riverside but *no* easy mooring. What Severn Way walkers lose over Ashleworth, they gain with this charming brick-built inn at the foot of Wainlode Hill. Tel: 01452 730251.

Connections

Service 351 operated by Swanbrooks (Tel: 01452 712386) links Haw Bridge Mon-Sat with Gloucester, Tewkesbury and Upton-on-Severn. Tel: 0870 608 2 608.

Ashleworth (Map 25)

There no longer being a ferry, walkers on the Severn Way are denied access to Ashleworth and its National Trust owned, but still agriculturally functioning tithe barn.

THE BOAT - riverside, mooring pontoon. Justly celebrated unspoilt pub which has been run by the same family for generations. Catering is restricted to lunchtime rolls and the varying choice of beer represents the output of many small local breweries whose ales come into their own at the pub's annual beer festival each autumn. Closed Mondays, and Wednesday lunchtimes. Tel: 01452 700272.

The Severn from Wainlode Hill

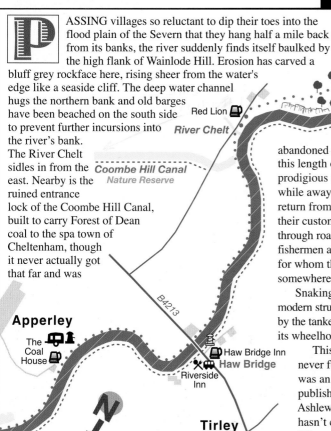

PASSING villages so reluctant to dip their toes into the flood plain of the Severn that they hang half a mile back from its banks, the river suddenly finds itself baulked by the high flank of Wainlode Hill. Erosion has carved a bluff grey rockface here, rising sheer from the water's edge like a seaside cliff. The deep water channel hugs the northern bank and old barges have been beached on the south side to prevent further incursions into the river's bank.

The River Chelt sidles in from the east. Nearby is the ruined entrance lock of the Coombe Hill Canal, built to carry Forest of Dean coal to the spa town of Cheltenham, though it never actually got that far and was abandoned as early as 1876. Old riverside inns punctuate this length of the river. Once they existed to quench the prodigious thirsts of the bargemen, or as somewhere to while away an hour or two waiting for the ferryman to return from poaching the squire's pheasants. Nowadays most of their custom comes from motorists who brave their way past 'no through road' signs, ramblers on the 'Severn Way' long distance footpath and the phlegmatic fishermen and elverers who seem to inhabit every reach. Plus, of course, the pleasure boater for whom these hostelries represent not only the source of welcome refreshment but also somewhere to moor on a river otherwise sadly lacking in such facilities.

Snaking in languid reptilian curves, the river comes to HAW BRIDGE, a relatively modern structure dating from 1961, having replaced an early 19th century bridge demolished by the tanker barge *Darleydale*. Coming 'in ballast', and thus high in the water, downstream, its wheelhouse collided with the bridge and the tanker skipper was killed.

This is Ivor Gurney country, the Gloucestershire poet and composer whose nerves never fully recovered from their exposure to the maelstrom of the trenches. The Severn was an important source of inspiration, as his first book of poetry *Severn & Somme*, published in 1917, confirms. In his following volume *War's Embers* the poem 'Above Ashleworth' appears, which speaks of the 'steady Severn silver and grey'. That, at least, hasn't changed. Sadly there is no longer a ferry linking Ashleworth with Sandhurst. Why were they considered so expendable - would a road bridge be closed so easily?

LONG Reach leads to Upper Parting. These old river names have an evocative resonance. And there were deeper subtleties: the navigable channel downstream of the Parting was known to working boatmen as 'Skipper's Length', whilst that above was known as 'Mates'. The tradition was that barge skippers would be at the wheel for the tortuous, narrow exit channel from Gloucester, being relieved once Upper Parting had been reached by the mate.

The now unnavigable western channel of the Severn, which loops past the village of Maisemore, was used to gain access to the Herefordshire & Gloucestershire Canal, a 34 mile rural waterway which took fifty years to build. Within forty years of completion in 1845 it had largely been converted into a railway. Twenty years ago no one would have considered that the H & G could ever be made navigable again, but other 'impossible' restoration projects have been achieved, and 'never' is no longer a word in any self-respecting canal activist's vocabulary. In recent years the junction basin at Over has

⚠ Advice for Boaters

1. On reaching Upper Parting, boaters are encouraged to telephone ahead to the lock-keeper at Gloucester - Tel: 01452 310832 - so that the lock into Gloucester Docks can be made ready for them.
2. Approaching Gloucester Lock beware the current drawing you towards the unnavigable channel to Lower Parting. The quay wall to your left has chains through which a line should be looped until the green light signals that you can enter the lock. Always attach your stern line first.

To City Centre

Victoria Basin

National Waterways Museum

Mariners Chapel

Llanthony Bridge
Tel: 01452 312143

Lock-keeper

Main Basin

Quay

drydocks

BW Office

Gloucester Lock
Tel: 01452 310832

White Horse (Chinese Rest.)

Gloucester

Cathedral

City Centre

Stonemason

Mean Ham

Docks

G&S CANAL

Gloucester Lock

Weir !

Port Ham

Upper Parting
Weir !

Alney Island

SEVERN WAY

Long Reach

Maisemore

Over

SEVERN WAY

Lower Parting

A38 to Bristol

A40

A417 to Ledbury

A40 to Ross

25

27

been cosmetically restored, though being on a tidal reach of the Severn it cannot be accessed by inland waterway craft.

The navigable, eastern channel of the Severn must have demanded all the barge skipper's fund of experience. If you have been used to the motorway breadth of the river down from Tewkesbury, this B-road backwater comes as something of a shock. It forms a surreptitious approach to the city, for the overhanging willows hide any view which might otherwise be had of the cathedral, but in its favour lies the fact that it ushers you into the very centre of the city without experiencing any of the drab outskirts which form an introduction to most towns and cities.

A series of bridges span the river as roads and railways converge on the city centre, before you reach the long wall of the old River Quay, where vessels which had navigated the tidal Severn used to berth prior to the development of the docks and the ship canal from Sharpness. Downstream of the Quay the river branches again, the right hand unnavigable channel leading round to Lower Parting. Head instead for Gloucester Lock, which dates from 1812 and was originally in the form of a staircase pair. Now it is one deep chamber, mechanised and spanned by a swingbridge carrying a busy road around the docks. As the lock fills, GLOUCESTER DOCKS are gradually revealed in all their grandeur and it is with a sense of exhilaration that you proceed into the Main Basin to seek out a mooring amidst these splendid surroundings.

Gloucester (Map 26)

Charles Dickens was amazed to find merchant seamen wandering conspicuously along the streets of what he imagined would be a quiet cathedral city. He followed one and discovered 'endless intricacies of dock and huge three-masted ships'. Naturally, there are no sailors to be followed today, and, in any case, one has one's reputation to consider. Also, most users of this guidebook will be wondering what Gloucester *itself* is like, having already become acquainted with the docks. In truth it's a bit of a curate's egg, a bit of a Mahler symphony, consisting of serene passages and alleyways interspersed with strident concrete shopping precincts. Here and there remains evidence of the Roman 'Glevum', stressing Gloucester's longevity. The city has, however, in its cathedral, a masterpiece of medieval architecture, an act of faith which transcends the shortcomings of modern life. Here is the largest stained glass window in England, the tomb of King Edward II and, in one shadowy corner, a moving memorial to a battalion of the Gloucestershire Regiment who made an heroic stand in the Korean War. Ignore the car parks and the concrete, this is the city's true testament.

Eating & Drinking
NEW INN - Northgate. Tel: 01452 522177. Rare example of a medieval galleried inn. Bar and restaurant food and accommodation. Local brews in the Ale Bar.
PREZZO - Southgate. Tel: 01452 414022. Part of a growing chain of modern restaurants where the emphasis is on pizza and pasta.
TOPOLY'S - Southgate. Tel: 01452 331062. Smart Italian near the docks.
YE OLDE FISH SHOPPE - Hare Lane. Tel: 01452 522502. Eat in or takeaway fish & chips etc.
SIR COLIN CAMPBELL - Llanthony Road. Tel: 01452 529615. Unprepossessing dockland pub of 1960s vintage but offering skittles and Arkells and bar food to west of docks.
The TALL SHIP (Wadworth) and the WHITESMITHS ARMS (Arkells) are both convivial dockland locals on Southgate yet both are sophisticated enough to offer food as well. In the redeveloped docks themselves are a wine bar and brasserie called FOSTER'S ON THE DOCKS and PIZZA PIAZZA.

Shopping
Tourists flock to the MERCHANTS QUAY shopping zone in the docks, you may wish to escape the water for a while and immerse yourself in the city centre shopping districts. Collectors of antiques will enjoy the ANTIQUES CENTRE housed in a former warehouse beside the entrance lock. On Westgate make for MADE IN GLOUCESTERSHIRE for indigenous crafts, gifts and food.

Things to Do
TOURIST INFORMATION - Southgate Street. Tel: 01452 396572.
NATIONAL WATERWAYS MUSEUM - Gloucester Docks. Tel: 01452 318200. Admission charge. The nation's premier waterways museum.
HOUSE OF THE TAILOR OF GLOUCESTER - College Court. Tel: 01452 422856. Shop and museum devoted to the world of Beatrix Potter.
CITY MUSEUM & ART GALLERY - Brunswick Road. Tel: 01452 396131. Roman and medieval displays, plus paintings, furniture, clocks etc.

Connections
TRAINS - services to/from Birmingham, London and Bristol and through the Golden Valley. Tel: 08457 484950.
TAXIS - Central Taxis. Tel: 01452 382020.

Gloucester & Sharpness

Cruising along the G&S near Slimbridge

THE Gloucester & Sharpness Canal's hitherto shabby departure from Gloucester Docks is likely to be transformed during the duration of this edition. In June 2006 British Waterways announced a multi-million pound regeneration scheme which would create a 'vibrant and colourful waterside where people can live, work and relax'. A thousand new houses, two thousand new jobs, and three million visitors a year are the predicted outcome from transforming sixty acres of decaying, post-industrial dockland. All very laudable, unless you happen to be an enthusiast of industrial archaeology and maritime heritage, in which case you will mourn the demise of all trace of the canal's vibrant commercial past: the docks and quays, the mills, warehouses and associated industries once sited specifically to take advantage of the transport facilities provided by the waterway.

Reactionaries can only pray that some of the more characterful buildings from the past are retained and put to sympathetic new uses. One thinks especially of the elegant 19th century Pillar Warehouses (Map 26), maltings. provender and flour mills which still lugubriously adorn the canal. Certainly the designers will have to do better than echo the aesthetic shortcomings of the bland retail park that previously replaced the vast Gloucester Railway Carriage & Wagon Works. A curious feature of the railway works were 'timber ponds' where logs used in the construction of rolling stock could be stored in the wet to prevent them from drying out and cracking prior to use; similar facilities were also provided for Gloucester's famous Moreland match factory.

Hempsted is the first of many swing bridges - operated by British Waterways keepers - which span the canal at regular intervals between here and Sharpness. Some two miles out, the canal has been rerouted to facilitate the construction of a new road and features a massive new swing-bridge of dual-carriageway proportions. The nearby hamlet of Stonebench is a good spot for viewing the Severn Bore.

Rea Bridge is graced by an ornately classical keeper's house, notable for its Doric-columned portico. These charming structures are to become increasingly familiar as the canal journeys south to Sharpness. North of Sellars Bridge the canal widens at the site of an oil terminal which received supplies by coastal vessels trading from South Wales until the early 1980s. The former quay iremains intact, incongruously backed by modern housing as though its denizens were in the habit of receiving all the paraphernalia of their modern lives by boat.

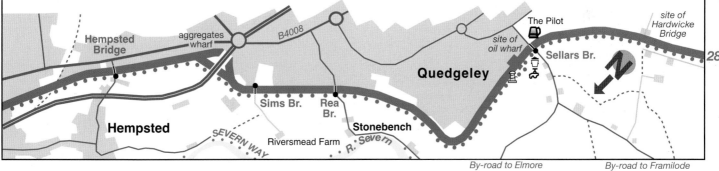

ACCOMPANIED by pylons and power lines, the Gloucester & Sharpness Canal traverses an apparently remote, low-slung landscape lost in a topographical void between the Cotswolds and the Forest of Dean. The fields focus on farms which, in their loneliness - and yours - assume a heightened significance. Between Parkend Bridge and Saul Junction the waterway is slightly elevated above the surrounding countryside with echoes of East Anglia in its reedy margins and reflections of high, wide skies. A derelict dumb barge lies moored listlessly to the towpath with a mock cargo of reeds and water. SAUL JUNCTION will once again be able to live up to its name when the ambitious Cotswold Canals restoration project is realised - see Map 31. The Stroudwater Canal predated the G&S by almost fifty years and was formally abandoned in 1954, though trade had ceased a dozen years earlier. Pending restoration, the junction

is still a fascinating location, and host to an increasingly well known annual waterways festival. Dominated by the high crane of a busy boatyard, conglomerations of moored craft resonate with its strategical past and there is much for the canal history devotee to imbibe, and their curiosity is catered for by a new Heritage Centre: solely refreshments are lacking; for them you'll have to walk to Frampton or Framilode.

At Fretherne Bridge you encounter a sizeable canalside flour mill which, in a previous existence, belonged to Cadburys. Waterbourne trade between here and the company's other premises at Blackpole (Map 20) and Bournville (Map 15) was once intensive; the last cargo of chocolate 'crumb' being carried from Frampton to Bournville by narrowboat circa 1961.

Frampton-on-Severn

B4071 from A38
M5 & Stroud

Frampton Court

Course of Stroudwater Canal

Wheatenhurst

By-road from A38

Parkend Br.

The Castle

Hardwicke Court

View to Cotswold Edge

Oakey Farm

Southfield Farm

SAUL JUNCTION

Davis & Son

former Cadbury works

Stroudwater Lock

Sandfield Br.
Heritage Centre

Fretherne Bridge

Course of Stroud-water Canal

27

Laynes Farm

View to May Hill

View to Forest of Dean

Epney

River Frome

Saul

SEVERN WAY

29

SEVERN WAY

Anchor Inn

Ship Inn

Framilode Lock

Framilode

River Severn

By-road to Longney

Frampton-on-Severn (Map 28)

Exiles and Anglophiles fantasise about villages like Frampton where Fair Rosamund (see Map 45) is reputed to have been born. Rosamund's Green incorporates a cricket pitch, duckponds and an array of horse chestnuts overlooked by a heterogeneous collection of houses from the large to the small, from the merely heavenly to the inherently sublime. Peacocks call from the 18th century purlieus of Frampton Court and many of the trees on the green have circular seats just made for watching the world go by.

Eating & Drinking

THE BELL INN - The Green. Tel: 01452 740346. Bistro, fish restaurant and afternoon teas.
THREE HORSESHOES - The Green. Tel: 01452 740463. Convivial village local with boule pitch to the rear.
JACQUELINE'S - The Green. Tel: 01452 740077. Pretty little restaurant open Wed-Sun for breakfasts, coffees, lunches and teas.

Shopping

Handsomely contained within a Georgian frontage, Frampton's excellent post office stores is obviously a focus of Frampton life. Wide range of provisions plus hot snacks for hungry walkers.

Connections

BUSES - 'Village Link' dial-a-bus service - Tel: 01452 423598.
TAXIS - Saul Taxis. Tel: 01453 826763

Contemplative break at Saul Junction

Epney (Map 28)

Severnside hamlet with a good pub called THE ANCHOR - Tel: 01452 740433. Also worth noting by Parkend Bridge is THE CASTLE (Tel: 01452 720328) a restaurant alongside the canal noted for its home-cooking.

Framilode (Map 28)

Back of beyond village with an interesting Victorian church overlooking the wide Severn. THE SHIP INN (Tel: 01452 740260) offers food and comes personally recommended by our publisher.

Saul (Map 28)

Shopless, publess, but not devoid of interest, particularly in that a number of its houses feature unusual friezes above their front doors. HERITAGE CENTRE - canalside Saul Junction. Cotswold Canals Trust adjunct to BW services block, open April-September, Sat, Sun & Bank Hols. Tel: 01285 643440.

HAVING acquired the mantle of the 'Severn Way', the canal continues its delightfully bucolic progress making its way past willow-fringed dykes draining fields extending down to the flood bank of the Severn, a seething, boiling mass of cafeteria tea-coloured water at high tide. Frampton's isolated parish church overlooks Splatt Bridge, whilst a ramshackle bungalow borders the entrance point to the once partially navigable River Cam, now used simply as a feeder to the canal. Such bungalows were a common feature of the Gloucester & Sharpness from the 1930s onwards. Built intially as holiday homes, many were gradually upgraded for domestic use throughout the year. Often self-built by their owners on land owned by the Sharpness Dock Company, some were actually constructed from materials brought along the canal by barge. Once there were almost a hundred of them, now less than half a dozen remain inhabited. To the north-west, far beyond the Severn, lies the landmark of May Hill, topped by a prominent clump.

Slimbridge is derived from 'slyme bridge', a reference to the once marshy nature of the surrounding landscape. The New Grounds are exactly that, land reclaimed from the river's tidal grasp during the 16th and 17th centuries. They provide rich pastures for cattle and once featured a number of decoys for the catching of duck. Nowadays, of course, it is with the preservation of duck and wildfowl that the area is concerned, since Peter Scott's establishment here of the Slimbridge Wildfowl and Wetland Trust in 1946. Son of the famous Antarctic explorer, Sir Peter Scott was the original Vice-President of the Inland Waterways Association, a close friend of Robert Aickman and one time husband of the novelist Elizabeth Jane Howard. In the early days of the Wildfowl Trust he brought a converted narrowboat called *Beatrice* to Shepherd's Patch to provide accommodation for visiting ornithologists. In 1950 *Beatrice* undertook a lengthy voyage of the northern canals as vividly described by Robert Aickman in *The River Runs Uphill*.

By-road from Cambridge & A38

By-road from Slimbridge & A38

feeder

Cambridge Arms Bridge

Glevum/ Slimbridge Boat Station

Shepherd's Patch

Tudor Arms

Ryall's Farm

41

Church End

Splatt Bridge

Patch Bridge

View to May Hill

New Grounds

SEVERN WAY

River Severn

Slimbridge Wildfowl & Wetlands Trust Centre

SEVERN WAY

View to Stinchcombe Hill

Hock Cliff

The Warth

28

30

T HE canal moves languorously through a landscape which feels as if it's about to fall off the edge of the globe. In the old days, perhaps, map-makers would have written "here be monsters" beyond the floodbank of the Severn: for all its proximity, the Forest of Dean might as well be on another planet.

Presently the canal curves round to Purton past a treatment plant which extracts its water on behalf of the population of Bristol. A pair of swing bridges (operated by a single keeper based at the lower bridge who uses CCTV) span the waterway as it winds around to the very edge of the Severn, whose banks are reinforced with the hulls of old barges berthed with a permanent cargo of silt and reeds. Reedy timber ponds and laid-up dredging craft ensue before you reach the remains of a swing bridge, which once carried a railway; not only over the canal, but over to the far side of the Severn as well! Opened in 1879, primarily to carry Forest of Dean coal across to Sharpness Docks, it consisted of twenty-one fixed arches spanning the estuary and a moveable arch, propelled by steam, over the canal. The cylindrical

base of the moveable arch, together with a couple of masonry arches on the opposite bank, are this astonishing structure's sole remnants. On a fog-bound October evening in 1960, *Arkendale* and *Wastdale,* two Harker petrol barges heading for Gloucester, missed the entrance to Sharpness Docks and collided with the bridge, demolishing one of the piers and bringing two of its girder spans down on themselves. Their unstable cargoes ingnited, and the blaze was worsened by the severing of a gas main on the bridge itself. Eyewitnesses described how the whole river was set alight. There were five fatalities from the barges, but things could have been worse, a group of contractors working on the bridge had clocked off early to listen to a Henry Cooper boxing bout on the radio. The railway never re-opened, and the remains of the two barges still lie off Purton. It would have been nice to know Sharpness when Tom and Angela Rolt moored *Cressy* here for 'a memorable month of summer' in 1948, and to have shared with them their train

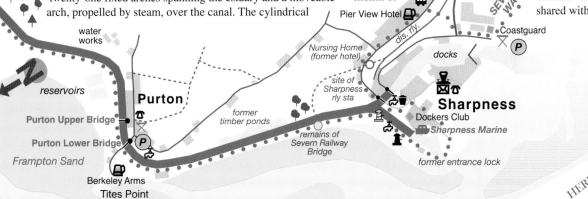

rides over the bridge to Lydney and the Forest of Dean. At that time there was considerable petroleum tanker barge traffic between Avonmouth and Worcester and Stourport, together with the occasional passage of a coastal vessel bound for Gloucester. Over the intervening half century cargoes have ebbed and flowed almost as furiously as the Severn itself, but the last regular through traffic was in the shape of Healing's barges, and their Indian summer finally died in 1998.

Not that Sharpness is a dead port now - far from it! Annual tonnage here is in the region of half a million - fertilizer from France, Germany and North Africa; cement from northern Spain; timber, paper coal, wheat and grain - though perhaps it neatly illustrates shortcomings in our balance of trade and manufacturing prowess that exports are restricted to scrap metal. Ships of up to 6000 tonnes are able to pass through the entrance lock - which has dimensions of 320 feet long by 57 feet wide - and if you want to see them you should position yourself at the picnic site on the south side of the approach jetty about half an hour before high water.

Nowadays the docks are operated by the Victoria Group, whose portfolio also includes Boston (Lincs), Bromborough (Wirral), Plymouth, and Seaham (Co. Durham). Since terrorism reared its ugly head, the innocent curiosity of by-standers is not encouraged, and pedestrian access to the dock precincts ends frustratingly at high-security fencing. Nevertheless, there are views to be gained from a number of vantage points, and considerable pleasure to be derived from simply sauntering amongst what areas remain of public access. On our most recent visit the *Monica Muller* had recently berthed with cement from Santander and our old friend, the classic passenger vessel *Balmoral* (on which we had once voyaged from Ilfracombe to Lundy) was enjoying a pre-season refit in the drydock.

The original course of the canal veers to the right, making its approach to the former entrance lock along an arm now used for moorings. Here, between 1939 and 1966 was berthed the mercantile training ship *Vindicatrix*, celebrated near the Dockers Club by a memorial erected in 2003. The original lock is closed now, but it enjoyed a brief new lease of life during the Second World War as an alternative point of entry in case of bomb damage. The lock apparatus from this period remains in place, the work of Cowans Sheldon, the Carlisle engineering firm perhaps better known for their railway cranes and turntables. A small detail, for sure, but emblematic of this resilient little port's abiding appeal.

Slimbridge (Map 29)

The village straggles down from the A38 to Shepherd's Patch, beyond which the road crosses the canal swing-bridge and makes a bee-line for the Wildfowl & Wetlands Trust centre. TUDOR ARMS - adjacent Patch Bridge. Tel: 01453 890306. Popular country inn with a good restaurant known far and wide for its 'Rorty Crankle' steaks. Local beers from Uleys and Wickwar. Accommodation.
Refreshments are also available at the WWT Centre and from a small cafe at the Boat Station. SLIMBRIDGE BOAT STATION - Patch Bridge. Tel: 01453 899190. Bike hire and day-boat hire facilities plus chandlery and cafe.

WWT SLIMBRIDGE - half a mile north-west of Patch Bridge. Tel: 01453 891900. Open daily year round, Slimbridge has the world's largest collection of rare and endangered ducks, geese and swans and offers brilliant views across the Severn from its observation tower.

Purton (Map 30)

Difficulty in mooring renders this a problematical stop for boaters, walkers being better placed to sample the BERKELEY ARMS (Tel: 01453 810291) an unspoilt pub tucked inconspicuously away between the canal and the river, though be warned of its idiosyncratic approach to pub hours.

Sharpness (Map 30)

A humbler counterpart to Goole on the Yorkshire Ouse, where life revolves around the enduring relationship between tides and docks. Scintillating views down the estuary to the Severn bridges and nuclear power plants. You are reminded of the centre forward's prerequisite - a certain Sharpness in front of Goole.
PIER VIEW HOTEL - in village to east of docks. Tel: 01453 811255. Food and accommodation. SHARPNESS DOCKERS CLUB - dock precincts. Tel: 01453 811477. Visitors can sign in.
POST OFFICE STORES in dock precincts and Co-op store in village.
BUSES - infrequent services to reality but not necessarily back again. Tel: 0870 608 2 608.

The Cotswold Canals

The Stroudwater Canal at Ebley

PENED in 1779, and measuring eight miles in length with thirteen locks, the Stroudwater Navigation enjoyed considerable prosperity before the Railway Age. And even thereafter, up until the Second World War, a moderate amount of local trade, predominantly in the guise of Forest of Dean mined coal, continued to use the route. Now it is due to be restored, along with the Thames & Severn Canal, at a cost approaching a hundred million pounds, to enjoy a new era of leisure-based boating. The first mile from Framilode to Saul Junction, however, is not to be made navigable again, because the Severn downstream from Gloucester is far too treacherous a river for inexperienced boat crews to be let loose upon. Thus this first section will remain the province of the walker who will be in a unique position to compare the characteristics of the waterway before

and after regeneration, and in doing so draw their own conclusions, however ambivalent they might be, concerning the Cotswold Canals' new lease of life.

Don't start off too quickly walking eastwards: contemplate the Severn; gaze across its broad expanse to the hilly outline of the Forest of Dean; pay a visit perhaps to St Peter's; then set your face towards the Cotswold escarpment - Sapperton Tunnel is almost twenty miles away and three hundred feet higher above sea level.

Framilode Lock was tidal and lies buried in a garden now. A reedy length of canal, more or less 'in water', runs past the Ship Inn, is culverted beneath the by-road to Saul, then promptly peters out as the path to Saul Junction follows the southern bank of the River Frome, channelled beside pollarded willows, to reach the Gloucester & Sharpness Canal at Saul Junction.

The first few hundred yards of the Stroudwater east of Saul remained in use as linear moorings after the navigation was officially abandoned in 1954. These end abruptly at the site of Walk swing-bridge. The by-road it carried from Wheatenhurst will need to be raised to provide navigable headroom when restoration takes place.

East of here sections of the canal have been obliterated, not least an aqueduct over the River Frome. It is planned to re-dig some of the original channel, but also to create a new line, so as to enable the canal to pass beneath the motorway where it crosses the Frome. Pending completion of this work, earmarked for 2010, walkers can follow at least some of the towpath as far as the site of Bristol Road Wharf before being forced into their own detour via the river bank. A fine hump-backed occupation bridge still spans this lily-rich stretch of water and two old pillboxes permit you to indulge in fantasies of invasion and resistance.

Fromebridge Mill has been converted into a popular pub and restaurant.

Walking beside the Frome would be an idyllic exercise but for the racket emanating from the M5, an immense and unceasing barrier of noise of El Alamein artillery barrage intensity. At least, in passing through the dark confines of the tunnel beneath the motorway, you can pretend to be a rock star emerging from your dressing room to a stadium filled with roaring fans.

Passing Meadow Mill you reach the northern outskirts of the village of Eastington and rediscover the original course of the navigation at Pike Bridge, rebuilt to navigational height in 2005. Dock Lock derived its utilitarian name from the presence of the Stroudwater company's boatyard and maintenance depot at this point. Pike Lock is overlooked by a cottage which latterly provided accommodation for a lock-keeper, but which originally - and hence its name - was a toll house on the local turnpike road.

Old occupation bridge near Bristol Road Wharf

BEYOND Pike Lock restoration has already been accomplished by the Cotswold Canals Trust as far as the Birmingham-Bristol railway. Blunder Lock is just that, having gained its amusing name from a miscalculation of water levels when the canal was being built. Newtown Lock was re-opened (in heavy rain) by the Prince of Wales in 1992. The towpath changes sides at Roving Bridge and proceeds to Bond's Mill Bridge, the world's first plastic lift bridge - sturdier than it sounds. Nice hill views are revealed to the south-east, down as far as Hetty Pegler's Tump!

On its high embankment, the main line railway presents an expensive challenge to the restorationists. A culvert of navigable dimensions will have to be inserted, and whilst this is not too difficult an engineering exercise, the fines imposed in disrupting rail traffic are likely to be costly.

Restoration of six miles of canal between 'The Ocean' and Brimscombe (Map 33) commenced in 2006, the former being a wide lily-filled pool which probably predated construction of the canal. This pretty scene is overlooked by Stonehouse Court, an extensive Elizabethan building renovated by Lutyens and now an hotel. Next door is the charming little church of St Cyr's which apparently relinquished part of its churchyard to the canal builders.

Two attractive houses abut Nutshell Bridge and are curiously linked by a passage beneath it. The route of the old Midland Railway line to Nailsworth crosses the canal on a cast iron bridge and there was once a transhipment wharf here. A private swingbridge spans the canal at Ryeford as the Cotswold Way swoops down on its hundred mile way from Chipping Campden to Bath.

Ryeford Locks are one of only two staircase pairs on the Cotswold Canals. Behind their isolated lock cottage you can see the unusual French Gothic church tower of Bodley's hillside church at Selsley. Ebley Mill provides a handsome landmark as the navigation nears Stroud. New housing is being erected along the canal bank; presumably such properties will derive added value from the canal's rebirth.

For details of facilities at Stonehouse see page 69

St Cyr's Church, Stonehouse

THE Stroudwater Navigation and Thames & Severn Canal meet at Wallbridge Basin on the outskirts of Stroud. The latter was completed across its astonishing summit in 1789, thereby linking two of Britain's greatest rivers and providing new transport opportunities for the manufacturers of the Forest of Dean and of South Wales, not to mention the cloth-makers of the Stroud Valley. Much celebrating took place on that November day towards the end of the 18th century, and will undoubtedly do so again when the Severn and the Thames are reconnected.

Altered in recent years by road building and redevelopment, Stroud's canalscape can only be improved by restoration. Sadly, though, no one has suggested bringing back the Stroud Brewery whose derelict coal chutes remain discernible between the locks. Another remnant of lost endeavour is the Midland Railway's blue brick viaduct which curves tantalisingly through the valley of the Frome, its last train having puffed into the sunset as long ago as 1949. In a contrast of fortunes, the former Great Western Railway viaduct remains in use, its tracks forming a close companionship with the canal all the way up to Sapperton.

Wallbridge Upper Lock is gated and makes a symbolic declaration of intent in the vanguard of further restoration. The railway spans a presently infilled section of canal and walkers are faced with a short detour past a Waitrose supermarket before regaining the canal as it regains its shape - though not as yet its depth - in a rewarding section stretching as far as Hope Mill Lock.

The Frome passes beneath the canal and establishes itself on the towpath side, broadening into a lagoon at the site of Arundel Mill. New housing overlooking Bowbridge Lock has had the wit to use local stone in deference to its location.

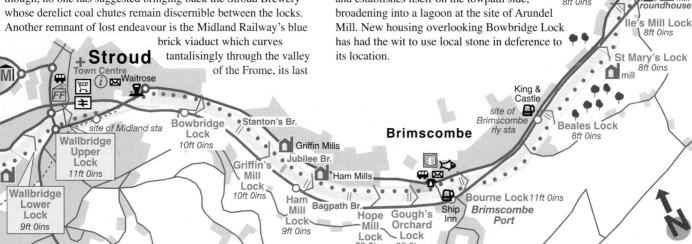

Remedial work carried out in the early days of the Cotswold Canal Trust in the 1970s has created the illusion of a working canal by Stanton's and Jubilee bridges. The latter is an attractive structure of cast iron latticework built to enable workers to reach the mills from their houses up on the hillside beyond the railway. The present day industrial premises along the valley floor perhaps lack the visual appeal of the earlier mills and one suspects that the majority of their workforces arrive and depart by road.

The pound above Ham Mill Lock is especially deep and photogenic in its proximity to the railway. Beyond Bagpath Bridge the canal bed grows thicker with reeds and then becomes infilled at the site of Hope Mill Lock. Briefly, by Gough's Orchard Lock, the canal line returns, but this proves just a brief illusion as Brimscombe Port is reached where a good deal of imagination is required to envisage the former layout of the canal and its associated wharves.

No avid canal enthusiast would have been immune to the fascination of Brimscombe in its heyday. The need for an inland port was brought about by the necessity of transferring goods between vessels of a different gauge: Severn 'trows' and Thames barges of the 'western' kind as well as a requirement to store items pending final delivery or further transport. Locks on the Stroudwater and Thames & Severn, though widebeam, were of differing dimensions, the former being 68/9ft long by 16ft 1/2ins wide, the latter originally 90-93 feet in length by 12ft 9ins or 13ft wide. To save water the Thames & Severn locks were reduced in length around 1841 and in the final years of trade carriers found the ubiquitous narrowboat a more suitable craft for working on the Thames & Severn than the wide-beam barges of old.

Brimscombe basin offered a hundred and seventy five thousand square feet of capacity and was said to have been able to accommodate up to a hundred vessels simultaneously. Notable features included the company's head offices, a transit shed, warehousing and a boat weighing machine used for establishing tolls. A central island was incorporated for the secure storage of goods which might, unprotected, have caught the attention of the thieving classes. The main warehouse found unusual use as a school following the demise of the canal and was unfortunately demolished in 1964. Thereafter, as so often is the case, the old port became an industrial estate. The most handsome survival is Port Mill, premises now of Tempus Publishing, whose list appropriately contains many titles devoted to the history of canals. Brimscombe will mark the eastern end of the inital restoration phase from Stonehouse (Map 32). Meanwhile walkers face a short detour (past a tempting fish & chip bar) before regaining the line of the canal by Bourne Lock, beyond which the canal is punctured again by the railway, following which it re-establishes itself as far as Chalford, a beguiling section upon which the Golden Valley begins to cast its spell.

A pub called the King & Castle recalls the existence of Brimscombe railway station alongside the canal. Here a small engine shed provided bankers for the climb to Sapperton summit. On to St Mary's, canal and railway - accompanied by the Frome chuckling transparently over it's clear gravel bed - create a mutually exclusive environment away from the traffic on the A419. An access lane to St Mary's Mill swoops down to cross the railway by way of a traditionally-gated level crossing guarded by a tiny signal box. Piped beneath the railway yet again, the canal briefly loses confidence before reappearing at Ile's Lock overlooked by a mellow and now domesticised Clayfield Mill, at least one occupant of which is proficient at the piano.

It grows increasingly difficult not to be overawed by the beauty of the canal's surroundings, as indeed was Temple Thurston on his famous (though perhaps over-imagined) voyage along the canal with the *Flower of Gloster* in 1910. He likened the surrounding scenery to Switzerland, something hacks are over-inclined to do when faced with precipitously hilly districts of England. Nevertheless his heart was in the right place and you too will be entranced by these 'blue slate roofs' viewed against a 'golden distance'. At Chalford you come upon the first of the Thames & Severn's keynote roundhouses and a gable end advertising 'James Smart - Coal, Stone & Sand Merchant, Dealer in Staffordshire Bricks'. Smart's barges traded here until abandonment finally took place in the 1930s; a priceless survival!

The Cotswold Canals
Before Restoration!

68

Stonehouse (Map 32)

Stonehouse will come into its own when boaters begin to use the Stroudwater Navigation once again. In the meantime, walkers will probably want to press on to Stroud where the facilities are closer to hand. Wycliffe College was founded in 1882. The remains of its original boathouse still stand beside the canal, though nowadays the boat crews are put through their paces on the Gloucester & Sharpness Canal at Saul Junction. In the 18th and 19th centuries, Stonehouse flourished, as other settlements along the Frome Valley, as a centre for the wool trade. Shops, banks, takeaways and other trappings of modern life are to be found in the vicinity of the railway station north of the canal.

Stroud (Map 33)

A codicil to the Cotswolds, with a spirited tradition of independent outlook, the textile town of Stroud tumbles down the valley side with the profile of a dry ski slope. Gradients apart, Stroud is a likeable place to wander around, several fine buildings vying for attention, none finer than the splendidly classical Subscription Rooms of 1833. In its heyday as a wool town Stroud was famous for its military tunics, now those mills left in production - out of the hundred and fifty which once functioned in the Frome Valley - are renowned for the production of snooker table baize and Wimbledon tennis ball felt.

Eating & Drinking

MILLS - The Shambles. Tel: 01453 752222. Pleasant wholefood cafe with pavement tables under a canopy within yards of where John Wesley preached from a butcher's block. WOODRUFFS ORGANIC CAFE - High Street. Exemplifies Stroud in both outlook and atmosphere; heavenly cakes!

LORD JOHN - Russell Street. Tel: 01453 767610. Wetherspoon conversion of post office, wide range of beer, good food and no intrusive music. THE BELL HOTEL - canalside Wallbridge Upper Lock. Tel: 01453 763556. Food and accommodation.

Shopping

Stroud's precipitous High Street is refreshingly bereft of chain stores (they lurk down in the ubiquitous Merrywalks Shopping Centre and can, as such, be left to their own anodyne devices) and congenially populated by individual retailers of more enterprising outlook, notably INPRINT (Tel: 01453 759731), a stylish secondhand bookshop with a choice collection of local subject matter. A few doors downhill lies STROUD BOOKSHOP, an increasingly rare example of an indepedently owned new bookdealer, whilst across the pedestrianised street is the window of a model shop which boys of all ages will find difficulty in resisting. MADE IN STROUD (Tel: 01453 758060) on Kendrick Street reflects the area's status as a haven for craftsmen and artists, and has links with the FARMER'S MARKET held in The Cornhill on the first and third Saturdays of each month.

Things to Do

TOURIST INFORMATION - Subscription Rooms, George Street. Tel: 01453 760960. THE MUSEUM IN THE PARK - Stratford Park. Tel: 01453 763394. Local heritage.

Connections

TRAINS - First Great Western services along the Golden Valley to/from Gloucester and Swindon with many through trains to/from London Paddington. Tel: 08457 484950. BUSES - Stagecoach services throughout the area, offering the opportunity of excursions to the likes of Dursley (a pretty market town); Wootton-under-Edge; or Slad (Laurie Lee country). Service No.54 threads its way through the Golden Valley via Brimscombe, Chalford and Sapperton to Cirencester Mon-Sat and is consequently of good use to towpath walkers. Tel: 0870 608 2 608. TAXIS - A&A. Tel: 01453 767777.

Brimscombe (Map 33)

Re-establishment of Brimscombe Port can only add lustre to this roadside settlement east of Stroud. Useful facilities for passing walkers include the SHIP INN (Tel: 01453 884388), KING & CASTLE (Tel: 01453 884388), a fish & chip shop, post office and newsagents.

Chalford (Map 33)

Cuddled in the lap of the Golden Valley, Chalford deserves to be savoured in its own right rather than just an adjunct to the canal. Indeed, there is something to be said for the walker detouring along the gorgeous by-road between Bell Lock and Golden Valley Lock to get a more intimate view of the higgledy-piggledy houses which define its character. The church of 1724 overlooks the canal roundhouse and features Pre-Raphaelite glass and 'Arts & Crafts' furnishings. Railway enthusiasts will remember Chalford as the eastern terminus of a push & pull service from Gloucester until 1964.

NEW RED LION - canalside above Bell Lock. Tel: 01453 882384. Friendly little pub with a cool interior. Beers include Wiltshire-brewed Moles from Melksham. Bar meals. POST OFFICE TEA ROOMS - Tel: 01453 882288. Post Office stores on by-road east of Bell Lock. Groceries and newspapers. Bike shop should your tyres or your ego need inflating. BUSES - Stagecoach service 54 runs Mon-Sat between Stroud and Cirencester calling also at Sapperton. Tel: 0870 608 2 608.

ENNINE overtones assail the Thames & Severn as it climbs through the Golden Valley. The Cotswold landscape is softer of course, yet you are still reminded of the constricted valleys of the Calder or the Colne, the Tame or the Roch. Here it was the course of the Frome which aided and abetted the canal builders, and the little river comes flowing transparently down its valley with the self-confidence of a child empowered by an important errand.

Thicker and thicker grow the locks, and the walker feels the climb, though not as much as the boaters will once navigation is restored. Clowes Bridge gained its name from the canal's resident engineer, Josiah, the man responsible for realising Robert Whitworth's blueprints in bricks and mortar. Narrowing, the constricted valley suffers lack of space, its hillside houses, so mellow, so apparently organic in origin, scattered haphazardly on shelves and terraces like the contents of a tiny corner shop.

With the railway - engineered by Isambard Kingdom Brunel, and opened to the Broad Gauge in 1845 -

intent on climbing harder, faster and attached to the neighbouring ridge on a remarkable sequence of blue brick viaducts (originally of typically Brunellian timber construction) the canal reaches Valley Lock, whereafter the houses and mills are largely left behind and woodland creates a very real sense of remoteness. In these very woods, while Eynsham Harry prepared a mid-day meal of wild hops, Temple Thurston counted seventeen varieties of wild flower. Short-changed by poetic impulse, Pearson was much more attracted to the redbrick and rounded windows of Chalford's erstwhile waterworks, enigmatic in decay. Dating from 1890, quite late in the canal's commercial career, coal for the furnaces was brought in by boat. On the towpath a milepost informs you that you have journeyed five miles from Wallbridge (Stroud) and that a further twenty-three and three-quarters remain to be

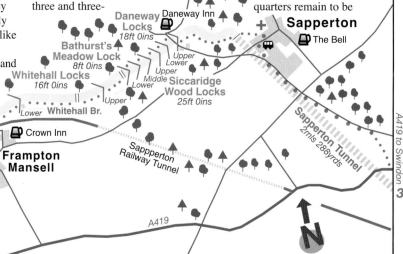

For details of facilities at Sapperton and Daneway see page 73

covered before reaching the Thames at Inglesham.

By Baker's Mill Upper Lock the Frome widens into a reservoir created by the canal company for water supplies. In doing so they were forced to acquire Puck's Mill in 1791 and close it down in order to guarantee a sufficient head of water. An inn once overlooked Puck Mill Upper Lock, an important thirst (and/or dragon) slayer on the long haul to the summit. Look out for a delightful (and occupied) dovecot attached to the end wall of a canalside house above the lock: footpaths splay off into the woods, begging to be explored.

The Golden Valley lives up to the implications of its name as the canal winds through woodland never out of earshot of the Frome. Walkers on the Thames & Severn towpath are joined at Whitehall Bridge by fellow travellers on the Wysis Way, a 55 mile path linking Offa's Dyke with the Thames Path. 'WD 1784' engraved on the arch of Whitehall Bridge refers to the mason William Dennis responsible for constructing this section of the canal. You are now entering the Sapperton Valley Reserve of the Gloucestershire Wildlife Trust and it is to be hoped that the return of boats does nothing to upset the fragile balance of flora and fauna in the vicinity.

Even in the canal's heyday, working up or down the final flight of seven locks to and from the summit at Daneway was often problematical given the paucity of water supply. Consumption was reduced by about 20% following shortening of the lock chambers. A series of sideponds had already been added in 1823, but every drop of water continued to count. By 1893 matters had grown so bad that the canal east of Chalford was closed. It re-opened six years later, but was still wracked by water problems. Encountering just one other boat (captained by an elderly lady humming quietly to herself at the tiller) Temple Thurston remarked that in places they barely floated at all, much to the chagrin of Fanny the boat horse. A quarter of a century later the author Geoffrey Boumphrey and a companion were unable to progress this far even by canoe as described in his book *Down River*, an account of a tour on the Severn and the Thames and, where possible, the Cotswold Canals, published in 1936. In the event Boumphrey and his pal 'George' had to portage their canoes by car between Chalford and Cricklade. They must have been reading William Bliss's, *Art and Practise of Canoeing on English Rivers, Navigations and Canals*, which records that he was charged 25 shillings to have his own canoe conveyed by road between Chalford and Cricklade!

The canal widened into a wharf and basin between the two Daneway locks, the upper of which was overlooked by an inn, once the Bricklayer's Arms now The Daneway. The higher lock has been infilled to provide the pub with a car park; future patrons of the beer garden will have the preferable ring-side view of an excavated lock chamber.

The summit lies 362 feet above sea level, but it rapidly becomes apparent as you twist in an easterly, becoming south-easterly direction away from Daneway, that the canal can go no further save by subterranean methods. And indeed, within less than half a mile, the neighbouring ridge rears suddenly up in defiance and the western portal of Sapperton is revealed, battlemented as if it means business; an entrance into Hades embowered by wild garlic.

3,808 yards long- impressive enough, but roundly beaten by the Huddersfield Narrow Canal's Standedge tunnel which is 5,698 yards long - and up to 200 feet below the surface of the Cotswold landscape it burrows through, Sapperton Tunnel was five years in the making. George III came to inspect it on Saturday 19th July 1788 as an antidote to taking the waters in nearby Cheltenham. Contemporary accounts suggest that His Majesty expressed astonishment. So, more practically, did Temple Thurston, who lay on his back with Eynsham Harry for four and a half sepulchral hours to propel the *Flower of Gloster* through the tunnel in time honoured fashion. In its working days a four-hourly cycle of entry times was the order of the day. A realisitic account of a boat being legged through the tunnel enlivens the opening pages of C. S. Forester's adventure *Hornblower and the Atropos*. Pending restoration, we have to walk across the top in the footsteps of the old boat horses and mules. For a heady moment one imagines that the dung on the road through Sapperton village is still steaming from those animals, until it becomes apparent that horse-riding is a popular activity amongst the rides of Oakley Wood.

WALKING over the top of Sapperton Tunnel gives you plenty of time to marvel at its existence - and perhaps yours as well. From time to time you catch sight of spoil heaps planted with beech trees which bring to mind all the activity of the human moles who dug the tunnel over two centuries ago Spare a thought too for the almost parallel railway tunnel completed in 1845 which is a mere 1 mile and 95 yards long. This is said to have been bored outwards from vertical shafts because the railway company wasn't yet in possession of the land at the ends of the tunnel!

If you were enamoured of the Gothic portal at the western end of the canal tunnel, you will probably be surprised to discover not a mirror image at the eastern end, but a design of quite different Classical style: a sort of double-A-side in pop single terms. It was restored by a local stonemason in 1977 and now waits only for boats to negotiate the summit for the first time since 1911. Above, and to the left of the portal, stands the Tunnel House Inn, erected during construction of the canal to provide accommodation and refreshment. It still fulfils the latter purpose admirably, though the original third storey was destroyed by a fire in 1952.

Recalling George III's visit, the cutting between the tunnel mouth and Tarlton Bridge is called 'King's Reach'. It is succeeded by the second Thames & Severn roundhouse encountered by westbound travellers. Coates Roundhouse differs from Chalford in two ways: it is (currently at any rate) uninhabited, but more significantly, its roof, though conical, is inverted, as a means of gathering rainwater for domestic use. Before the railway arrived it must have been a lonely

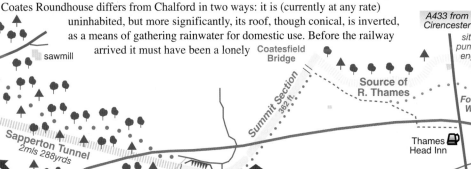

36

Park Leaze
Bridge

site of
Smerrill
Aqueduct

Halfway
Bridge

site of
former
rly Bridge

By-roads to Ewen

Course of G.W.R.
Cirencester Branch

A433 from
Cirencester

site of
pumping
engine

R. Thames

Thames Path

Fosse
Way

A419 from Stroud

sawmill

Coatesfield
Bridge

Source of
R. Thames

Summit Section
362 ft.

34

Sapperton Tunnel
2mls 288yrds

Thames
Head Inn

Tunnel
House
Inn

Tarlton
Bridge

Coates
Roundhouse
(ruin)

The Tavern

Kemble

Course of G.W.R.
Tetbury Branch

A433 to Tetbury

A429 to Malmesbury

location for the resident company employee and his family. Forcibly closed by the local authority on health grounds in the 1950s, it now resembles an abandoned lighthouse, especially as glimpsed from passing trains.

The summit section of the Thames & Severn is 8 miles 13 chains in length. Sadly the canal east of Sapperton is not so well defined as in the Golden Valley. At Coatesfield Bridge it ceases to be a right of way and walkers are forced to join a field path which soon passes the official Source of the Thames. Meanwhile the canal encounters the Roman Road which links Lincoln with Exeter, the famous Fosse Way, and comes upon the site of a pumping house which, in its various guises ranging from a windmill, through a Boulton & Watt beam engine to a second-hand steam pump from a Cornish mine, supplied three million gallons of water a day to the summit until 1912. The last engine was scrapped as part of the war effort in 1941, though the rebuilt pumphouse remains, off limits and in domestic use.

Walkers, unfortunately, miss all this, their route lying to the south along the Thames Path as far as the enchanting village of Ewen, beyond which they rejoin the canal at Halfway Bridge, alongside a three-arched, stone-built bridge which formerly carried the Kemble-Cirencester branchline over a by-road and the canal. Halfway Bridge marks the halfway point of the Thames & Severn Canal and it was rebuilt in 1997, a small, yet important gesture which kept up the impetus of the canal's eventual restoration. However charming the Thames, especially in its transparent, strippling state, it feels good to be re-united with the canal, which for half a mile or so, is convincingly defined, if predominantly as dry as the stone walling which delineates its towpath side from neighbouring farmland. How the rabbits who make its dry banks their home, or the rooks who nest in the high tops of trees which overhang the canal will react to an invasion of dumper-drivers and membrane-layers is anyone's guess, but nature has a ready knack of making restitution. Presently, it becomes necessary to detour on to the adjacent by-road as the towpath becomes impassable and the canal bed peters out. Circencester Council used the canal as a linear refuse tip in less enlightened times: one trusts that any surviving councillors have the grace to express regret in what must now be their dotage.

Sapperton (Map 34)

Idyllic settlement perched above its famous tunnel offering easy access to view the western portal. Historic links with proponents of the Arts & Crafts movement. Unfortunately no shops, but a very good pub called THE BELL (Tel: 01285 760298). Buses to Cirencester and Stroud - Tel: 0870 608 2 608.

Daneway (Map 34)

Hamlet at the head of the Golden Valley best known in canal circles for its eponymous canal boatmen's pub the DANEWAY INN (Tel: 01285 760297) a charming Wadworth house previously called the Bricklayers Arms when the canal was open. CAMRA recommended and a good (if slightly over-priced) menu.

Kemble (Map 35)

Over the years, housing schemes have enlarged Kemble, whose prime role had hitherto been as host to the railway junction of the branchlines to Cirencester and Tetbury, the latter famous for its isolated station called Trouble House Halt which featured in Flanders & Swann's elegiac song *Slow Train*. The branchlines and their railbuses have gone now, but the splendid Tudoresque station remains a popular railhead for this well-heeled district - 'Paddington - 81 minutes' as the house advertisements put it in *Country Life*!

Eating & Drinking
TUNNEL HOUSE INN - adjacent eastern portal of Sapperton Tunnel. Tel: 01285 770280. Idyllically located inn once visited by John Betjeman and his father.

Shopping
The Post Office stores in village centre is the only shop anywhere remotely close to the canal between Chalford and Siddington.

Connections
TRAINS - excellent service linking Swindon with Gloucester and Cheltenham. Stroud is a comfortable 15 mile walk away. Tel: 08457 484950.

BUSES - connections with Cirencester and Tetbury. Tel: 01285 653985 or 01452 425543. TAXIS - Tel: 01285 642767.

AT Bluehouse you can detour to see a former lengthsman's cottage, but otherwise your way lies via public footpaths and by-roads to Siddington, site of the former junction of an arm which led into Cirencester itself and the beginning of the mainline's descent to the Thames at Inglesham. The majority of the arm lies beneath an industrial estate now. Another Whitchurch, another Leek; enlightenment deepening the regret that the lines of their canals have been lost beneath hasty redevelopment.

The quartet of locks at Siddington lower the canal by almost forty feet, the lowest being buried beneath a new house

which provocatively carries a narrowboat on its name plaque. One imagines it will have to be moved or demolished to effect restoration unless they fancy a cellar with a working lock chamber as a conversation piece. Between the third and the fourth chambers, another transport casualty, less likely to be revived, is the Midland & South Western Railway, one of those wonderful cross country lines of no apparent use to anyone but railway enthusiasts, though this line, which linked Cheltenham with Southampton, did bizarrely flourish briefly as a route for northerners bent on emigrating to Australia.

Cowground Bridge is intact and of traditional hump-back appearance. It is followed by the remains of a swing-bridge, and then the Thames & Severn crossed the River Churn: the original masonry aqueduct has been replaced in recent years by a wooden footbridge. The Churn rises high up on Cotswold to the south of Cheltenham and has its confluence with the Thames at Cricklade. It was one of a baker's dozen of tributaries lyrically described by the poet and topographical writer Brian Waters in his *Thirteen Rivers to the Thames* published by Dent in 1964. In it he noted that water-mills are as frequently encountered on the Thames and its tributaries as public houses along an English road: forty years

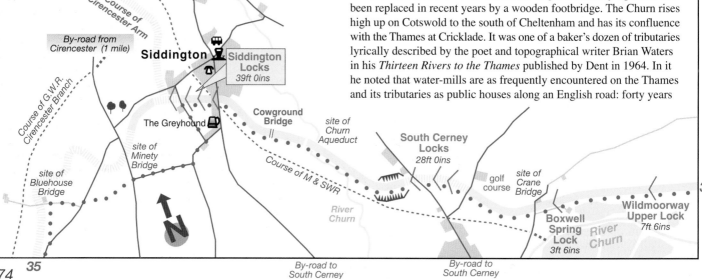

By-roads from Cirencester (1 mile)

Course of Cirencester Arm

By-road from Cirencester (1 mile)

Siddington

Siddington Locks
39ft 0ins

Course of G.W.R. Cirencester Branch

The Greyhound

site of Minety Bridge

site of Bluehouse Bridge

Cowground Bridge

site of Churn Aqueduct

Course of M & SWR

River Churn

South Cerney Locks
28ft 0ins

golf course

site of Crane Bridge

Boxwell Spring Lock
3ft 6ins

River Churn

Wildmoorway Upper Lock
7ft 6ins

N

By-road to South Cerney

By-road to South Cerney

Ruined Roundhouse

of contestable progress have not dealt kindly with this observation. There is still, however, if you look closely enough, evidence of a fascinating irrigation system which once permitted the meadowlands beside the Churn to be deliberately flooded in winter so as to protect the grass beneath from freezing and also to allow rich nutrients in the river water to enhance the grazing properties of the meadows the following spring. A seat commemorating Councillor David Fox, a keen advocate of restoration, offers the chance to dally in such delightful surroundings. Close your eyes and imagine the approaching clip clop of a boat horse, a dripping towline, and a western Thames barge laden with Cotswold stone whilst, to your rear, the South Express (through carriages Liverpool Lime Street to Southampton) shuffles past in a vapoury dream of soot and oil.

Claymeadow Cutting precedes South Cerney Wharf where locally baked bricks once provided regular cargoes. The wharf house remains in domestic use. Will its owners welcome a canal on their doorstep? All three locks in the South Cerney flight are buried but should provide no undue difficulties in re-establishing them. Crossing the road, one walks at 45 degrees across a field overlooked by one of Gloucestershire's many wartime aerodromes, regaining the line of the canal at Northmoor Lane where a new golf course provides ramblers and canal enthusiasts with interesting contrasts in the use of leisure time. A pleasant length of canal follows, though the increasing decibels of 'noises off' earmark the impending intrusion of a busy dual-carriageway. The well preserved chamber of Boxwell Spring Lock is a mere 3ft 6ins deep. It wasn't originally intended that there should be a lock here at all, but a miscalculation in water levels rendered its construction a necessity. The towpath progresses through an avenue of ivy-clad tree boles to Wildmoorway Upper Lock where rotting tail gates lie submerged within inky black pools of brackish water.

UITE apart from the canal's present state of dereliction, the 18th or 19th century boatman would be hard pressed to recognise his surroundings, the present landscape of flooded gravel workings bounded by the busy A419 trunk road, not being one which he would either be familiar with nor necessarily comfortable in. The character of the 21st century manifests itself most strongly below Wildmoorway Lower Lock where a new spine road, car park and picnic site encourage road-based visitors to enjoy the charms of the Cotswold Water Park: leisure for the masses needs to be ring-fenced and manufactured now. At least the road bridge has been rebuilt pending restoration.

Tall reeds swaying in the shallow waters of the canal mask the visual, if not the aural, impact of the main road as the towpath forms the boundary between Gloucestershire and Wiltshire. Cerney Wick Lock is overlooked by the third of the Thames & Severn's five roundhouses; as at Chalford the roof points conically upward. The lock chamber has top gates but the adjoining road bridge is levelled and the canal culverted beneath. Across the Churn The Crown offers an opportunity for refreshment and meditation.

Latton Basin marked the junction of the Thames & Severn and North Wilts canals for a number of years. The North Wilts opened in 1819 and created a nine-mile link with the Wilts & Berks Canal at Swindon, its chief benefit lying in its ability to provide a more reliable route to Abingdon than via the rather less than reliable upper Thames, though its gauge was constrained by a dozen narrow locks. Formally abandoned in 1914, though

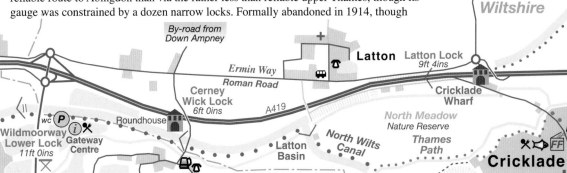

denuded of trade long before that, the North Wilts ironically provides present day walkers with the best option for progress pending restoration, because the Thames & Severn between Latton and Inglesham is for the most part infilled and no longer a right of way. A solid path follows the dry bed of the North Wilts to the banks of the Thames where the Thames Path can be joined for an enjoyable onward walk via Cricklade to Inglesham, a distance of approximately ten miles. Diehards may progress along the line of the Thames & Severn to Cricklade Wharf, but the A419 compromises much of the original canal bed and it is a matter of walking along a desultory access road, too close to the noisy dual-carriageway to be considered enjoyable.

Cricklade Wharf retains its original, and imposing, Thames & Severn wharf building, but it turns its rear to the road and is off limits to the general public. Frustratingly the best view is from the A419, and that, by definition, a fleeting glimpse. The basin at Cricklade Wharf was infilled long ago but a major victory was achieved by the canal lobby when the A419 dual carriageway was constructed with a navigable culvert in 1997. Beyond Cricklade we would advocate use of the Thames Path or an alternative route promulgated by Gerry Stewart in his equally practical and lyrical book *The Cotswolds Canal Walk (ISBN* 0 952787 03 2) which recommends a network of public footpaths via Down Ampney, Marston Meysey and Kempsford.

Cricklade (Map 37)

The ancient Wiltshire town of Cricklade is dominated by the turreted 16th century tower of the parish church of St Samson of Dol. Otherwise, one main street defines the town, sloping from the Jubilee Clock of 1897 steadily, widely, and agreeably down to the Town Bridge over the Thames past St Mary's, Britain's 'oldest Catholic church'. A small museum celebrating the town's rich history opens on Wednesday and Saturday afternoons.

Eating & Drinking

RED LION - foot of High Street. The first pub on the way into town from the Thames Path and difficult to better. Moles ales and guests, Tel: 01793 750776. Food and accommodation. CAMRA recommended.
WHITE HART HOTEL - High Street. Tel: 01793 750206. Old coaching inn offering Swindon-brewed Arkells, food and accommodation.
CRICKLADE CAFE - High Street. Tel: 01793 750754. Filling food for famished walkers.
CROWN INN - Cerney Wick. Tel: 01793 750369. Popular pub offering food and accommodation on the edge of the Cotswold Water Park and within easy reach of the towpath.
GATEWAY CENTRE CAFE - Tel: 01285 862962. Open daily 10am-4pm.

Shopping

Facilities include a pharmacy, Tesco Express, and a Lloyds TSB bank with cash machine, but best of all is MICHAEL HART'S butchers shop (Tel: 01793 750213) which purveys championship-winning sausages, pies and pasties, not to mention oven-ready pheasants.

Connections

BUSES - Stagecoach and Thamesdown services to/from Swindon and Cheltenham via Cirencester. Tel: 0870 608 2 608.

Restored Roundhouse

SHYNESS, as already hinted, overcomes the Thames & Severn between Cricklade and Inglesham, and until restoration takes place it is not feasible for members of the general public to follow the line of the canal in a satisfactory, let alone enjoyable manner. There are, however, one or two highlights that the diligent explorer will find of interest. A public footpath affords access to the site of Marston Meysey Wharf, private property now but retaining an overbridge and a roundhouse which has been tastefully incorporated into a modern dwelling. Enjoy a view of it, by all means, but respect its new owner's privacy as with all such mementoes of the canal in its prime. Old maps are required to make sense of the canal's eastward progress, the next convincing proof that it passed hereabouts being Oatlands Bridge, a high and dry remnant in a field close to the road on the outskirts of Kempsford.

According to David Viner's invaluable *The Thames & Severn Canal - History & Guide* (ISBN 0 7524 1761 4), at least one of its bricks is embossed with the name of the Stonehouse Brick & Tile Co, evidence surely of materials being conveyed by boat along the line of the canal, if not for construction, then at least for maintenance in later years.

Kempsford lies on the Thames, and the two watercourses lay closely parallel for some distance, though nowadays, owing to access constraints, the Thames Path runs away from the riverbank in this locality. When the Thames & Severn was first being surveyed, consideration was given to making its junction with the Thames here rather than at Inglesham. Long ago the river formed the boundary between Mercia and Wessex at this point - now it contents itself with dividing Glos. from Wilts.

Wharf Lane reminds villagers that they once had a canal on their doorstep, and one imagines that most of them will be glad to have it back, not least the landlords of the village's two pubs. East of Kempsford the canal continues infilled and all but invisibly on the last lap to its junction with the Thames at Inglesham.

Marston Meysey

Old Speckled Cow

roundhouse

Oatlands Bridge

RAF Fairford

By-road from Fairford

Axe & Compass
The George

Kempsford

Ham Barn

River Thames

37

Red Lion

Castle Eaton

Wiltshire

Gloucestershire

Thames Path

By-road to Highworth

By-road to Highworth

The Upper Thames

Nearing Lechlade

OVERLOOKED by the last of its five characteristic roundhouses, the Thames & Severn Canal and River Thames meet at Inglesham a mile upstream of Lechlade. As a declaration of intent, Inglesham Roundhouse was purchased by British Waterways in 2003 to pave the way for restoration. It is intended that in due course it will be available for holiday hire, and it is difficult to think of a more appealing dwelling for those of an inland waterway bent seeking a peaceful retreat for a week or two.

Inglesham is generally recognised as the head of navigation on the River Thames as far as motor vessels are concerned, yet, legally, small unpowered craft such as canoes can get as far upstream as Cricklade. But as far as this guide is concerned, we concentrate now on the Upper Thames, and in particular the thirty lonely, twisting, shallow but very lovely miles between Lechlade and Oxford, one of the most rewarding inland waterway experiences in Britain.

As befits the largest - indeed the *only* - town on the upper reaches, Lechlade has been shaped, commercially and culturally by the presence of the Thames on its doorstep. Today a marina provides boating activity where once stone and cheese and wool were the prevalent cargoes. Lechlade or Halfpenny Bridge dates from 1793, its colloquial name derived from the toll paid by pedestrians (unless they could convince the toll-keeper that they were bound for the church!) until 1839. Downstream the Thames essays a charming course overlooked by the spacious customer moorings of the New Inn, and the soaring Perpendicular spire of St Lawrence, together with a number of gracious private gardens, some sporting elegant gazebos. Informal public moorings are available on the south, Wiltshire bank of the river against a wide expanse of watermeadows. Idyllic indeed!

Map labels

River Coln

Dudgrove Farm

Thames & Severn Canal

38

Inglesham Lock
6ft 2ins
Inglesham Roundhouse

70'

Dudgrove Double Lock
11ft 6ins

Gloucestershire

River Thames

Thames Path

Thames Path

Wiltshire

Lechlade Marina

Lechlade

Thames Path

P Lechlade Bridge

River Cole

Oxon.

St John's Bridge

The Trout

St John's Lock
2ft 10ins
Tel: 01367 252309

Oxon.

River Leach

Oxon.

Glos.

Cotswold Hire

40

A361 to Swindon

* Allow 1 hour for navigable section between Inglesham and St John's Lock

St John's Lock is the highest on the Thames, but if you travel all the way to Teddington you will arguably be unable to find one better tended. It is graced by a reclining statue of Father Thames, postcards of which are obtainable from the lock-keeper. It is the work of R. Monti and was sculpted for the Crystal Palace in 1854. Between 1958 and 1974 it graced the source of the Thames at Thames Head, but was prone to the attention of philistines and vandals, and this lockside was considered a safer spot for the old man's contemplation of his river.

Downstream of the lock cut two Thames tributaries join the channel: the River Cole, from the south flows off the Marlborough Downs below Swindon and forms the boundary between Wiltshire and Oxfordshire; the River Leach rises high up on the Cotswolds, lends its name to the Fosse Way village of Northleach, and travels fifteen miles to meet the Thames - once it was said to yield 'the finest watercress in England' which was loaded on to a train each evening at Lechlade station for transit to Covent Garden.

Lechlade   (Map 39)

Cause or effect ? - it would be difficult to manufacture a more amenable town to accompany the head of navigation on the River Thames. Formerly at the meeting place of four counties, Lechlade graces the south-eastern corner of Gloucestershire with thoroughfares of mellow 'Cotswold' stone. Cricklade and Cirencester have their towers, perfectly Perpendicular St John's at Lechlade has its spire, a landmark amongst the watermeadows for miles. Shelley came here in 1815 (having rowed all the way from Old Windsor!) and wrote a poem about it - its gargoyles are remarkable! As befits a visitor-orientated town, rowing boats and motor boats are available for hire, as are bicycles Tel: 01367 253599.

Eating & Drinking

NEW INN - Market Square. Tel: 01367 252296. Old coaching inn offering bar and restaurant meals and accommodation. Customer moorings at the foot of its lengthy garden.
COLLEYS SUPPER ROOMS - High Street. Tel: 01367 252218. Elaborate six-course dinners and Sunday lunches for discerning gourmets.
J A FLONG - Market Square. Tandoori

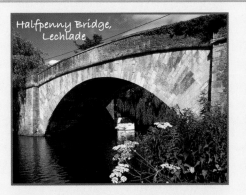

Halfpenny Bridge, Lechlade

restaurant and takeaway. Tel: 01367 252956.
RED LION - High Street. Tel: 01367 252373. Arkells, steaks and accommodation.
BLACK CAT TEAROOMS - High Street. Cafe/restaurant. Tel: 01367 252273.
THE CAFE - Market Square. Tel: 01367 253990. Upstairs cafe over a wine merchant plus pavement tables for warm days.
THE RIVERSIDE - Thames Street. Tel: 01367 252229. Popular riverside pub.
MONICA'S PLAICE - High Street. Tel: 01367 250050. Eat in or take-away fish & chips etc.

THE TROUT - riverside St John's Bridge. Tel: 01367 252313. One of three 'Trouts' on the Upper Thames. Bar and restaurant meals, nice big garden, customer moorings.

Shopping

A LONDIS minimarket (offering 'cashback' on purchases) is located in the Market Square and provides most day to day necessities, though there is also a butcher and delicatessen and wine merchants with an exceptionally good choice of bottled beer. There's also a pharmacy, post office, and a branch of Barclays bank. Several antique, craft and gift shops provide counterpoint to day to day requirements, notably a shop selling Christmas goods all year round!

Connections

BUSES - since the closure of its railway station back in the Sixties, there is regrettably (and irrationally) no longer a public transport link with Oxford. There are, however, reasonable bus services to/from Swindon and Cirencester - Tel: 0870 608 2 608.
TAXIS - CT's. Tel: 01367 252575.

CCASIONALLY, in its inexperience, this youthfully navigable Thames coils itself up like a mischievous hose pipe, producing fiendishly difficult bends for the steerers of anything longer than a cabin cruiser to deal with. From the relative safety of the Thames Path, ramblers can watch the less-adept's attempts to extract themselves from sandbanks with feigned concern and hidden glee: it was always thus. But whether walking or boating, or simply picnicking on its banks, there is no escaping the inherent beauty of the river, nor its capacity for filtering out the less admirable excesses of 21st century living.

Parcels of land at Buscot are within the care of the National Trust. The riverside parsonage can be visited, though only by prior appointment. Its car park occupies the site of a wharf where, amongst other items, local cheese was despatched by barge to Oxford and London. Frustratingly, however, all trace of the vast Berkshire Distillery which stood upstream of the lock, has vanished.

Brainchild of Robert Campbell, the mid 19th century Australian denizen of Buscot Hall, and part of his 'great agricultural experiment', whereby the estate was intensively farmed for the production of sugar beet, distilled into alcohol and exported to France for brandy making. Another endeavour was a brick and tile works which had its own wharf at the end of a short canal off the main river channel.

Eaton Footbridge marks the site of the last flash lock on the river, extant until as relatively recently as 1937. It was operated by an arcane arrangement of 'rymers' and 'paddles' far too complicated to unravel here. A pub called The Anchor overlooked the river here until it burnt down with loss of life in 1979.

But it is perhaps Kelmscott Manor which is the cynosure on the reach between the locks at Buscot and Grafton. Sixteenth century in origin, with its mellow stonework masked from the river by a raucous high-rise community of rooks, it is inevitably for its associations with William Morris and the Pre-Raphaelites that the house is valued now. Morris arrived here in 1871, initially sharing the manor with Dante

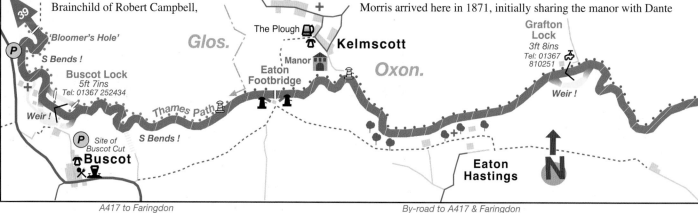

Gabriel Rossetti who paid rather too much attention to Jane Morris (who sat for many of his best known paintings) for the household's equilibrium. A man of tremendous energy - political activist, forward thinker, designer of wallpapers, stained glass windows and furniture, early supporter of the Arts & Crafts movement, founder of the Society for the Protection of Ancient Buildings, and writer of poetry and prose - Morris employed Kelmscott as a summer retreat for quarter of a century and relished in particular its proximity to the Thames, alongside which his busy workaday life was spent at Hammersmith. His Utopian work of fiction, *News From Nowhere*, describes a dream-voyage upstream from London to Kelmscott (in 2003), encountering above Oxford 'whispering beds of reeds and willows dipping into the stream'. He must, presumably lie most contentedly in Kelmscott churchyard alongside his wife Jane and daughters.

The Pre-Raphaelites busied themselves hereabouts: the tiny church at Eaton Hastings features glass by Burne-Jones. Grafton lock is typical in its remoteness. Opened in 1896 it had to wait until 1960 to receive the benefit of electricity.

Buscot (Map 40)

A model settlement dating from 1879, thankfully unimpinged upon by the A417, though you will have to brave its verges should you wish to visit the National Trust's Buscot House. The Old Parsonage is also a NT property, though only accessible by written request. The village shop may offer meagre provisions, but in its role as a tea room, with tables in the garden, it would be difficult to beat. BUSCOT HOUSE - Tel: 01367 240786. 18th century neo-classical house set in fine parkland 1 mile south-east of the river. Generally open April to September Wed-Sun.

Kelmscott (Map 40)

Morris's opinion that Kelmscott represents 'heaven on earth' is not much wide of the mark. His beloved Manor House is managed by the Society of Antiquaries and flings its doors open to an appreciative public on Wednesdays and Saturdays from April to September - Tel: 01367 252486. Refreshments are available at such times and a shop deals in Morris memorabilia. The PLOUGH INN (Tel: 01367 253543) has flagstone floors - always a reassuring sign - and offers food and accommodation. Les Routiers recommended.

Buscot Backwater

A plethora of drainage dykes and channels serves to emphasise how marshy this district once was. Predominantly flat and just over two hundred feet above sea level, it is a profoundly strange parcel of emptiness despite its proximity to Oxford and Swindon. Second World War fortifications provide a surreal accompaniment to the river which, like the Kennet & Avon Canal twenty miles to the south, was perceived as a strategic line of defence in the event of a German invasion. They look foolish now and inadequate, but conflict is always just around the corner, as the war planes flying out of Brize Norton to the north all too frequently and frighteningly confirm. One feels safer with antiquities such as Radcot Bridge, 13th century in origin and generally regarded as the oldest on the Thames, though possibly predated by a Saxon structure. All of which is academic to boaters, who pass beneath an upstart new bridge engineered by William Jessop in 1790 as part of improvements to the Upper Thames carried out in conjunction with the opening of the Thames & Severn Canal. With its humped-back and simple single arch, it has all the hallmarks

of a canal bridge, but its location on a double bend, requires care and concentration from steerers. The old navigation channel has been adopted for private moorings.

Radcot Lock is exceptionally pretty. From Old Man's Bridge you can walk along blissful lanes to the mellow little town of Bampton, a centre for morris Dancing. In 1954 an American B47 bomber crashed beside the river in mysterious circumstances during the Cold War.

Sequences of sharp bends characterise the river's progress between Radcot and Rushey locks: narrowboat captains have their work cut out to follow the channel; walkers are tempted to cut corners! The steeple of Bampton church plays hide and seek with you on the reach between Rushey and Tadpole Bridge. The towpath changes sides, becoming a metalled access road to Rushey Lock. Tadpole Bridge was built in 1802 and consists of a single arch. A coal wharf once presented a busy scene where moorings are now provided beside the Trout Inn.

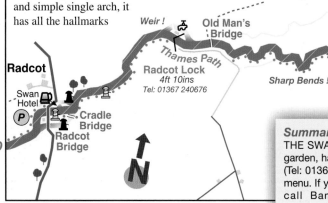

Weir ! Old Man's Bridge
Thames Path
Radcot Lock
4ft 10ins
Tel: 01367 240676
Sharp Bends !

Rushey Lock
6ft 0ins
Tel: 01367 870218
Sharp Bends !
Weir !

Thames Path

Tadpole Bridge
Trout Inn

Radcot
Swan Hotel
P
Cradle Bridge
Radcot Bridge

40

N

A4095 to Faringdon

Upper Thames Cameos

THIS, you'll discover in due course, is an altogether different Thames from the floating-gin-palace-infested waters of the middle river. Thank Oxford's low-slung Osney Bridge for that, as well as the restricted depth and convoluted nature of the upper reaches, and the fact that the majority of boaters feel more at home in the lowest common denominator comfort zone of Henley and Windsor. Up here, in highest common factor country, perseverance and initiative are rewarded by an absence of crowds, the only likely observers of your progress being geese and swans and sheep. It also becomes apparent why the upper Thames bargemen of the 19th century favoured the North Wilts and Wilts & Berks canal route between Cricklade and Abingdon over this narrow and winding watercourse. Pollarded willows frame the river's course pleasingly - electricity pylons less so. Cattle stoop to drink where the banks have become eroded into sandy bays: it's all very bucolic and satisfyingly remote.

The Thames hereabouts used to form the boundary between Oxfordshire to the north and Berkshire to the south. Regrettably, it is Oxon. on both banks now: topic for discussion - is change invariably a dynamic for good, or a chronic human mechanism designed to compensate for inactivity? We oscillate from reorganization to reorganization, yet remain as far as ever from the rainbow's end of perfection.

Shifford derives its name from 'sheep ford' and was once a much busier spot than the farm and Victorian chapel encountered today. Alfred the Great held a parliament here in 885. Shifford Lock is the youngest on the river, having been opened in 1898 as part of a new cut by-passing the lengthy loop through Duxford, though small craft may still explore this side arm up as far as the old ford itself. The Thames Path adopts this route as well, temporarily deserting the river east of Tenfoot Bridge.

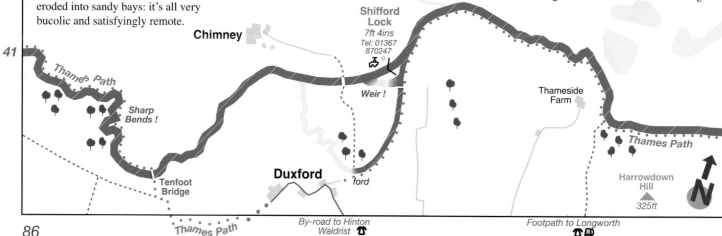

T can be disorientating to discover the Thames flowing *north* as is the case in the vicinity of Bablock Hythe. Without the natural obstacle of Cumnor Hills, it might have missed Oxford entirely (and where would the dark blue boat crew then be ?) and headed directly for the sea via Abingdon, only half a dozen miles from Bablock Hythe by road, but nearly twenty by water. Ideally you need copies of Matthew Arnold's *The Scholar Gypsy* and *Thyrsis* with you, lengthy mid-19th century poems which echo the mellow, elegiac beauty of the Upper Thames: 'Or in my boat I lie, Moor'd to the cool bank in the summer heats, 'Mid wide grass meadows which the sunshine fills,' are lines which boaters can readily relate to. The Scholar Gypsy crossed the stripling Thames at Bablock Hythe, and so too can present-day walkers as long as the ferry, owned by the landlord of The Ferryman Inn (Tel: 01865 880028) is operating. Quite what Matthew Arnold, let alone Thyrsis, would make of the caravan park which

lines the riverbank at Bablock Hythe, is probably best not dwelt on. Less intrusive, are the dwellings with boathouses which line what was formerly the Berkshire bank of the river south of Northmoor Lock. Marked by four tall poplar trees, Northmoor Lock dates from late 19th century improvements to the Upper Thames. Footpaths lead from this isolated spot to the villages of Appleton and Northmoor. Similarly, each village can be reached from Hart's Footbridge, the site of an old flash weir. A mid 18th century weir-keeper's daughter here was wooed and won by an aristocratic Oxford undergraduate. They married in Northmoor Church in 1766.

Newbridge illustrates the folly of ever calling anything 'new'. New Bridge is the second oldest on the river, dating from the middle of the 13th century, and being *continued overleaf*

R. Windrush

Newbridge
The Rose Revived

A4 15 to Abingdon

2

Thames Path

By-road from Stanton Harcourt

44

Bablock Hythe

The Ferryman
ferry (seasonal)

Public right of way from Northmoor

Northmoor Lock
4ft 1in
Tel: 01865 862923

Thames Path

Weir !

Public footpath to Appleton

For details of facilities at Appleton, Newbridge and Bablock Hythe see page 88

'new' only in relation to Radcot. The River Windrush has its source near Bourton-on-the-Water up in the Cotswolds, and flows down through Burford and the blanket-making town of Witney. Wilson MacArthur wrote a book about it, published by Cassell as part of a series of river-following books, after the Second World War, when, grateful for having held on to what we might well have lost - as a nation and as individuals - there was still a market for such homespun topographical titles. Now we prefer our vicarious travels to be conducted ideally in more exotic climes. It would be pleasant to lean over the lichened parapet of one of its upstream facing arches, watch the waters of the Windrush adding their weight to the Thames, and consider the scene here in 1644 when Cromwell's troops captured the bridge from the Royalists following the briefest skirmish, were the Abingdon to Witney road not so busy nowadays. The Thames Path detours away from the river north of Bablock Hythe, returning by Farmoor Reservoir. If the ferry is operating, walkers have the option of using it to cross the river and continue along the former towpath on the east side of the river, rejoining the Thames Path at Pinkhill Lock.

Newbridge (Map 43)

THE MAYBUSH - riverside (south bank), customer moorings. Tel: 01865 300624. Convivial riverside pub vying for trade with its better known rival on the opposite bank. Good bar meals.

THE ROSE REVIVED - riverside (north bank), customer moorings. Tel: 01865 300221. Hugely popular, this spacious and historic inn attracts a wide variety of patrons from far and wide. Bar and restaurant food; gondola hire in the summer months.

Bablock Hythe (Map 43)

Up until 1965 the ferry was capable of carrying road vehicles, offering a useful shortcut between Cumnor and Stanton Harcourt.

THE FERRYMAN INN - riverside. Tel: 01865 880028. Another famous Upper Thames hostelry continuing to trade on its historic reputation. Bar and restaurant food, and accommodation. Tea dances and music hall shows! Operators of the ferry in summer months.

For a quieter pint, try the Red Lion *in Northmoor - Tel: 01865 300301*

Swinford Toll Bridge

BUSES - Stagecoach service No.18 offers Mon-Sat links with Oxford and Bampton, making this a useful staging post for Thames Path walkers - Tel: 01865 772250.

Appleton (Map 43)

Sleepy village on the old Berkshire side of the Thames accessible on foot from Northmoor Lock. Post office stores and a pub called the PLOUGH INN (Tel: 01865 862441).

Eynsham (Map 44)

Picturesque and soporific, Eynsham is a worthwhile walk along a pavemented road from the Thames at Swinford Bridge. Shops, pubs and takeaways (though no bank as far as we could see) give you an excuse for the exercise involved.

Closer to the river, you'll find the TALBOT INN -Tel: 01865 881348 - a comfortable Arkells pub offering both food and accommodation.

Bus service 100 operates at quarter of an hour intervals between Eynsham and Oxford (half-hourly on Sundays).

LOW-BANKED, and at its most northerly, the Thames arcs around the poet Matthew Arnold's 'green-muffled' Cumnor Hills. Deciduously wooded, and roamed by deer, Wytham Hill rises to 539 feet, the highest point of the Cumnor 'range'. One of the Thames's most gorgeous tributaries, the River Evenlode, makes its entry a little over a mile downstream of Eynsham Lock. The Evenlode's source lies near Stow-on-the-Wold and flows down through the remnants of the ancient Forest of Wychwood. It was too shallow and meandering a river ever to be practically navigable, but at the beginning of the 19th century, the Duke of Marlborough

funded the construction of Cassington Cut, a canal not quite a mile long, mainly to serve the mill at Cassington but also as an outlet for Eynsham malt. It was last used around 1870, but remains a useful drainage channel. Cassington was a 'halt' on the Oxford to Fairford railway. Predominantly hauled by 'Pannier' tank locomotives, the last passenger train trundled off stage forever in 1962, though the line had experienced unprecedented busyness during the Second World War, bringing men and materials to the army camps and military aerodromes in the area. Paul Jennings wrote wistfully about its demise in *Just A Few Lines*, long

out of print but reasonably easily obtained secondhand.

SWINFORD TOLL BRIDGE was built in 1777 and many consider it one of the most handsome on the Thames. Three of its nine honey-coloured stone arches span the water. A classically-styled toll house abuts its northern approach, but the keeper spends most of his time in a plastic shelter nowadays, bamboozled by levels of road traffic that the 18th century Earl of Abingdon can never have envisaged when he bought out the ferry and commissioned William Taylor to design the bridge. Much of Oxfordshire derives its water supplies from Farmoor Reservoir which in turn draws its water from the Thames.

Map labels

Eynsham — The Talbot
Swinford Toll Bridge
Pinkhill Lock 3ft 6ins Tel: 01865 881452 Weir !
Eynsham Lock 2ft 9ins Weir ! Tel: 01865 881324
B4044
Anglo-Welsh/ Oxford cruisers
waterworks
Cassington Cut
R. Evenlode
Course of Fairford — Oxford Rly
former station (closed 1962)
Thames Path
pumping station
Farmoor
Wytham Great Wood
Thames Path
Farmoor Reservoir
P
B4017 to Abingdon
B4044 to Oxford
A40 to Oxford

KING'S LOCK, depending on your direction of travel, is the first or last on the Upper Thames to be hand-operated - Godstow, in contrast, is mechanised. Just upstream of King's, a backwater leads to the Duke's Cut offering access (for boaters, *not* walkers) to the Oxford Canal. Working narrowboats passed through the Duke's Cut until the 1950s with Warwickshire coal for the paper mills at Wolvercote.

Godstow Lock is overlooked by the ruins of a 12th century nunnery indelibly associated with Rosamund Clifford, the 'Fair' mistress of Henry II. When the lock cut was being dug workmen disturbed the bones of long departed nuns.

The Thames' entry into Oxford (or exit from) is magnificently made along the banks of Port Meadow against a backdrop mostly consisting of 'dreaming spires' with one or two less salubrious 21st century additions. Between Godstow and Binsey the reach is often busy with schoolboy rowing fours and eights accompanied by the sharp but cultured megaphone assisted bark of sports masters.

A second opportunity to make for the Oxford Canal comes via the Sheepwash Channel upstream of Osney's low headroom bridge (7ft 6ins max): full details of the canal are to be found in *Pearson's Canal Companion to the Oxford & Grand Union Canals,* whilst the Thames downstream of Osney as far as Brentford is covered in the *Kennet & Avon + Middle Thames Canal Companion.* Whichever route you decide to take, great adventures await you, but you will find nothing more lovely than the Upper Thames.

A43 from Brackley

Oxford Canal from Banbury

BICESTER

Hotel

Service Area

OXFORD

The Parks

Banbury Rd.

Dukes Lock
5ft 4ins
232

234

The Plough
235 236

St Edward's School

239A

238

239

The Anchor

Woodstock Rd.

St. Giles

Broad St.

High St.

Cathedral

Covered Market

City Centre

Folly Br.

233

Dukes Cut Lock

Duke's Cut

Wolvercote Lock
3ft 8ins

240
park

242

Walton St.

College Cruisers
50'

Louse Lock
3ft 6ins

Castle

St. Aldates

FF

Wolvercote

OXFORD CANAL

243

70'

memorial

Port Meadow

Rowing !

Sailing !

Thames Path

RIVER THAMES OR ISIS

Sheepwash Channel

Weir !

Sharp Bends !

A34

Trout Inn

Weir !

Bossoms
The Perch

Osney Bridge

Osney Weir !

King's Lock
2ft 6ins
01865 553403

Thames Path

Godstow Lock
5ft 2ins
01865 554784

Nunnery (ruin)

Weir !

Low Headroom !

Osney Lock
6ft 3ins
01865 553403

Binsey

44

*Figures relate to River Thames between King's Lock and Osney Lock

Oxford (Map 45)

Oxford's pressures seem not so much 'Town & Gown' nowadays, as 'Town & Tourism'. Yet it can still remind you of an exclusive club, where the best the casual visitor can do is press their nose up against the lattice windowpane and peer enviously at the academically privileged world revealed within. Like Thomas Hardy's hero, we are all 'Obscure Judes', in awe of this world-renowned seat of learning. In Oxford - perhaps more than in any other English city - time stands quite literally still. Whole quadrangles and cloisters seem frozen into a medieval eternity where only the undergraduates ubiquitous bicycles break the chronological spell. From the perspective of the river boat, or the open-topped tourist bus, the sightseer can derive a vicarious wisdom. After all, you can now truthfully recall: "When I was at Oxford."

WATERMANS ARMS - riverside above Osney Lock. Tel: 01865 248832. Cosy local, bar food.

LAMB & FLAG - St Giles. Ancient inn associated with C.S. Lewis and Tolkien and, in recent years, one Endeavour Morse. Lunchtime food. Tel: 01865 515787.

THE NOSEBAG - St Michael's Street. Tel: 01865 721033. Long established wholefood cafe/restaurant.

THE PERCH - Thames-side, Binsey. Thatched riverside inn set back behind a mask of trees. Large garden, wide menu. Tel: 01865 240386.

THE TROUT - adjacent weir channel at Godstow. Arguably the most famous of the three Upper Thames 'Trouts'. Foaming weir and foaming pints. Wide range of food. Tel: 01865 554485.

BROWNS - Woodstock Road. Tel: 01865 319655. Well established brasserie converted from former Morris garage.

BANGKOK HOUSE - Hythe Bridge Street. Tel: 01865 200705. Thai restaurant, bear right at canal end.

LOCH FYNE - Walton Street. Tel: 01865 292510. Fishy chain in Jericho.

LE PETIT BLANC - Walton Street. Tel: 01865 510999. Raymond Blanc owned restaurant hidden away in the backstreets of Jericho and enjoying its tenth anniversary in 2006.

RESTAURANT ELIZABETH - St Aldates. An Oxford institution, predominantly French cooking. Tel: 01865 242230.

Shopping

Drawing on a wide range of custom and taste, Oxford's shops are inspired to an admirable eclecticism. The COVERED MARKET (off High Street) hosts the most wonderful cross-section of retailers. As befits a seat of learning, there are some good bookshops, though not, sadly, as many secondhand and antiquarian outlets as in Betjeman's and Larkin's days.

Things to Do

TOURIST INFORMATION - Broad Street. Tel: 01865 726871 *www.visitoxford.org*

CITY SIGHTSEEING - open top bus rides with running commentary. Regular departures from the railway station and city centre stops. Tel: 01865 790522.

THE OXFORD STORY - Broad Street. Ride through Oxford's rich history. Tel: 01865 728822.

MUSEUM OF OXFORD - St Aldates. Tel: 01865 815559.

ASHMOLEAN MUSEUM - Beaumont Street. Tel: 01865 278000. Britain's oldest public museum (not Mons) displaying European, Egyptian and Near Eastern antiquities.

CARFAX TOWER - Carfax. 99 steps to heaven for a bird's eye view of the city of dreaming spires.

PUNT HIRE - Oxford's most traditional means of seduction can be hired from boat houses at Folly Bridge on the Thames and Magdalen Bridge on the Cherwell.

COLLEGES - over thirty colleges make up Oxford University. Many of them are world famous such as Balliol and Merton which are both of 13th century origin; Magdalen (pronounced 'Maudlin') which dates from 1458; and Christ Church founded in 1525 by Cardinal Wolsey. The general public may look around most of them in the afternoons.

OPEN SPACES - much of Oxford's charm rests in the proliferation of green spaces, the city's lungs. These include: The Parks, Christ Church Meadow and Port Meadow. A stroll - or a picnic -on any of them comes as a refreshing experience after the hurly burly of the main thoroughfares and helps put Oxford in the context of its riverside setting.

TRAINS - services along the Thames Valley to/from Reading and London and connections to/from the midlands and the north. Tel: 08457 484950.

BUSES - service 100 runs four times an hour across the road from the railway station to Eynsham, but to reach Lechlade you will need to continue to Witney and change. Tel: 0870 608 2 608.

TAXIS - Radio Cars. Tel: 01865 242424.

How to use the Maps

There are forty-five numbered maps whose layout is shown by the Route Planner inside the front cover. Maps 1 to 7 cover the River Avon; Maps 8 to 13 cover the Stratford Canal; Maps 14 to 20 cover the Worcester & Birmingham Canal; Maps 21 to 26 cover the River Severn; Maps 27 to 30 cover the Gloucester & Sharpness Canal; Maps 31 to 39 cover the yet to be restored Cotswold Canals; and Maps 39 to 45 cover the upper reaches of the River Thames.

The maps are easily read in either direction. The simplest way of progressing from map to map is to proceed to the next map numbered from the edge of the map you are on. Figures quoted at the top of each map refer to distance per map, locks per map and average cruising time. An alternative indication of timings from centre to centre can be found on the Route Planner. Obviously, cruising times vary with the nature of your boat and the number of crew, so quoted times should be taken only as an estimate. Neither do times quoted take into account any delays which might occur at lock flights in high season or against strong current conditions on the river sections.

Using the Text

Each map is accompanied by a route commentary, and details of most settlements passed through are given close by. Regular readers will already be familiar with our somewhat irreverent approach. But we 'tell it as we find it', in the belief that the users of this guide will find this attitude more valuable than a strict towing of the tourist publicity line.

Towpath Walking

The simplest way to go canal exploring is on foot. It costs largely nothing and you are free to

Information

concentrate on the passing scene; something that boaters are not always at liberty to do. Unfortunately the same cannot always be said of rivers where, down the centuries, landowners have cordoned off many ancient rights of way. The Avon is a typical case in point, significant sections of its banks being inaccessible to pedestrians. Thankfully, the Severn and the Thames are now accompanied by long distance paths, though again there are sections out of bounds to the general public, making detours necessary. In the course of preparing this guide we have walked every yard of the relevant towpaths and a good proportion of the river paths and can thoroughly recommend them as a means of getting to know these inland waterways without a boat. As usual the maps show the quality

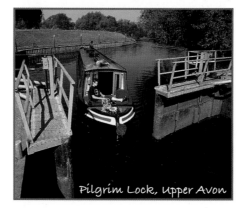

Pilgrim Lock, Upper Avon

of the towpath, and whilst it does vary from area to area, none of it should prove problematical for walkers.

Towpath Cycling

Cycling canal towpaths is an increasingly popular activity. At present it is theoretically necessary for cyclists wishing to use towpaths to acquire a free of charge permit from a British Waterways office - see opposite page for appropriate addresses. Cycling on the river paths is not formally encouraged and the surface, in any case, rarely conducive to a pleasurable journey.

Boating

Boating on inland waterways is an established, though relatively small, facet of the UK holiday industry. There are over 25,000 privately owned boats registered on the canals, but in addition to these numerous firms offer boats for hire. These range from small operators with half a dozen boats to sizeable fleets run by companies with several bases. Most hire craft have all the creature comforts you are likely to expect. In the excitement of planning a boating holiday you may give scant thought to the contents of your hire boat, but at the end of a hard day's boating such matters take on more significance, and a well equipped, comfortable boat, large enough to accommodate your crew with something to spare, can make the difference between a good holiday and an indifferent one.

Traditionally, hire boats are booked out by the week or fortnight, though many firms now offer more flexible short breaks or extended weeks. All reputable hire firms give newcomers tuition in boat handling and lock working, and first-timers soon find themselves adapting to the pace of things 'on the cut'. Turn to page 94 for contact details of boat hire operations.

Navigational Advice

LOCKS are part of the charm of inland waterway cruising, but they can be potentially dangerous environments for children, pets and careless adults. Use of them should be methodical and unhurried, whilst special care should be exercised in rain, frost and snow when slippery hazards abound. We lack space for detailed instructions on lock operation: trusting that if you own your own boat you will, by definition, already be experienced in canal cruising; whilst first-time hire boaters should be given tuition in the operation of locks before they set out. Briefly, however, those new to these cruising waters should note that the locks on the Stratford and Worcester & Birmingham canals are of the narrow variety and pose no undue difficulties, whereas the locks on the rivers Avon, Severn and Thames are of widebeam dimensions and thus capable of taking narrowboats side by side. Landing stages are provided up and downstream of each chamber to enable crews to get on and off their craft. In widebeam locks boats should be secured with lines fore and aft once they are in the lock chamber to prevent them being buffeted by turbulence as the lock fills or empties. The locks on the River Severn are automated. A guide to boating on the River Severn and the Gloucester & Sharpness Canal is obtainable from BW in Gloucester. On the Upper Thames all the locks are usually manned. Their telephone numbers appear on our maps. We recommend boaters on the Thames acquire a copy of the Environment Agency's *A User's Guide to the River Thames*.

MOORING on the canals featured in this guide is per usual practice - ie on the towpath side, away from sharp bends, bridge-holes and narrows. An open bollard symbol represents visitor mooring sites, either as designated specifically by British

King's Norton Junction

Waterways or, in some cases, as recommended by our personal experience or that of our regular correspondents. Of course, one of the great joys of canal boating has always been the opportunity of mooring wherever (sensibly) you like. In recent years, however, it has become obvious that there are an increasing number of undesirable locations, particularly in urban areas, where mooring is not recommended for fear of vandalism, theft or abuse.

CLOSURES (or 'stoppages' in canal parlance) traditionally occur on the inland waterways between November and April, during which time most of the heavy maintenance work is undertaken. Occasionally, however, an emergency stoppage, or perhaps water restriction, may be imposed at short notice, closing part of the route you intend to use. Up-to-date details are normally available from hire bases. Alternatively, British Waterways provide a recorded message for private boaters, the number to ring being: 01923 201402. Information is also available on BW's internet site at *www.british-waterways.org*

Useful Contacts

BRITISH WATERWAYS
Stratford and Worcester & Birmingham canals - British Waterways, Central Shires, Peel's Wharf, Fazeley, Tamworth, Staffs B78 3QZ. Tel: 01827 252000.
River Severn, Gloucester & Sharpness Canal, Cotswold Canals - British Waterways, Harbour House, West Quay, Gloucester Docks, Gloucester GL1 2LG. Tel: 01452 318000.
British Waterways operate a central emergency telephone service - Tel: 0800 47 999 47.
RIVER AVON
UPPER AVON NAVIGATION TRUST / LOWER AVON NAVIGATION TRUST - Mill Wharf, Mill Lane, Wyre Piddle, Pershore, Worcs WR10 2JF. Tel: 01386 552517 *www.shakespearesavon.co.uk*
RIVER THAMES
Environment Agency, Kings Meadow House, Kings Meadow Road, Reading RG1 8DQ Tel: 0845 601 5336 *www.visitthames.co.uk*
The Inland Waterways Association was founded in 1946 to campaign for retention of the canal system. Many routes now open to pleasure boaters may not have been so but for this organisation. Membership details may be obtained from: Inland Waterways Association, PO Box 114, Rickmansworth WD3 1ZY.
Tel: 01923 711114 *www.waterways.org.uk*
Cotswold Canals Trust is an affiliation of bodies determined to see the Stroudwater Navigation and Thames & Severn Canal restored to navigable status to effect a broad beam link between the Severn and the Thames. Tel: 01285 643440 *www.cotswoldcanals.com*
Stratford-on-Avon Canal Society
www.stratfordcanalsociety.org.uk
Worcester & Birmingham Canal Society
www.wbcs.org.uk

Hire Bases

ALVECHURCH BOAT CENTRES - Alvechurch, Worcs & Birmingham Canal, Map 16. Tel: 0870 8352525. One of seven bases. *www.alvechurch.com*

ANGLO WELSH - Tardebigge, Worcs & Birmingham Canal, Map 17, Wootton Wawen, Stratford-on-Avon Canal, Map 9 and Eynsham, Upper Thames, Map 44. Tel: 0117 304 1122. One of ten bases. *www.anglowelsh.co.uk*

BIDFORD BOATS - Bidford, River Avon, Map 6. Tel: 01789 773205. *www.bidfordboats.co.uk*

BLACK PRINCE HOLIDAYS, Stoke Wharf, Worcs & Birmingham Canal, Map 17. Tel: 01527 575115. One of six bases. *www.black-prince.com*

BROOK LINE - Dunhampstead Wharf, Worcs & Birmingham Canal, Map 19. Tel: 01905 773889.

COLLEGE CRUISERS - Oxford, Oxford Canal, Map 45. Tel: 01865 554343. *www.collegecruisers.com*

COTSWOLD BOAT HIRE - Lechlade, River Thames, Map 39. Tel: 01793 727083. *www.cotswoldboat.co.uk*

EVESHAM MARINA - Evesham Marina, River Avon, Map 4. Tel: 01386 768500. *www.cascadas.co.uk*

GLEVUM BOAT HIRE - Slimbridge, Gloucester & Sharpness Canal, Map 28. Tel: 01453 899190 *www.slimbridgeboatstation.com*

SHERBORNE WHARF - Birmingham, Map 14. Tel: 0121 455 6163. *www.sherbornewharf.co.uk*

STARLINE NARROWBOATS - Upton-on-Severn, River Severn, Map 23. Tel: 01684 592140. *www.starlinenarrowboats.co.uk*

VIKING AFLOAT - Worcester, Worcs & Birmingham Canal, Map 20. Tel: 01905 610660. One of four bases. *www.viking-afloat.com*

Boating Directory

Boatyards

BOSSOM'S BOATYARD - Oxford, R. Thames, Map 45. Tel: 01865 247780.

BREDON MARINA - Bredon, River Avon, Map 1. Tel: 01684 773166.

R. W. DAVIS & SON - Saul, Gloucester & Sharpness Canal, Map 28. Tel: 01452 740233.

HANBURY WHARF - Worcs & Birmingham Canal, Map 18. Tel: 01905 771018.

LECHLADE MARINA - Lechlade, River Thames, Map 39. Tel: 01367 252181.

FRANK LYONS - Warstock, Stratford-on-Avon Canal, Map 13. Tel: 0121 474 4977.

JOHN PINDER & SONS - Worcester & B'ham Canal, Stoke Prior, Map 17. Tel: 01527 876438.

OXFORD CRUISERS - Eynsham, River Thames, Map 42. Tel: 01865 881698.

SANKEY MARINE - Evesham, River Avon, Map 4. Tel: 01386 442338.

SEABORNE LEISURE - Kempsey, River Severn, Map 21. Tel: 01905 820295.

SHARPNESS MARINE - Sharpness, Gloucester & Sharpness Canal, Map 30. Tel: 01453 811476.

STRENSHAM MILL - Strensham, River Avon, Map 2. Tel: 01684 274244.

SWALLOW CRUISERS - Hockley Heath, Stratford-on-Avon Canal, Map 11. Tel: 01564 783442.

TEWKESBURY MARINA - Tewkesbury, River Avon, Map 1. Tel: 01684 293737.

UPTON MARINA - Upton-on-Severn, River Severn, Map 23. Tel: 01684 594287.

WELFORD BOAT STATION - Welford, River Avon, Map 6. Tel: 01789 750878.

WESTERN ROAD MARINA - Stratford-on-Avon, Stratford Canal, Map 8. Tel: 01789 263772.

WYRE BOATYARD - Wyre Piddle, River Avon. Map 3. Tel: 01386 751897.

Day Boat Hire

ANGLO WELSH - Wootton Wawen, Stratford Canal, Map 9. Tel: 01564 793427. Tardebigge, Worcester & Birmingham Canal, Map 17. Tel: 01527 873898.

BANCROFT CRUISERS - Stratford-on-Avon, River Avon, Map 7. Tel: 01789 269669.

COTSWOLD BOAT HIRE - Lechlade, River Thames, Map 39. Tel: 01793 727083.

DROITWICH CANAL CO - Ladywood, Droitwich Barge Canal. Tel: 01905 458352.

GLEVUM - Gloucester & Sharpness Canal, Map 29. Tel: 01453 899190.

HANDSAM - Evesham, River Avon, Map 4. Motor and rowing boats. Tel: 01386 834070 or 07860 895416.

OXFORD CRUISERS - Eynsham, River Thames, Map 42. Tel: 01865 882235.

RIVERSIDE - Lechlade, River Thames, Map 39. Motor and rowing boats. Tel: 01367 253599.

Trip Boats

AVON BOATING - Trips on the Avon at Stratford, Map 7. Tel: 01789 267073.

AVON LEISURE CRUISES - Trips on the Avon at Evesham. Tel: 01386 860988.

BANCROFT CRUISERS - Trips on the Avon at Stratford, Map 7. Tel: 01789 269669.

BICKERLINE - Trips on the Severn at Worcester, Map 20. Tel: 01905 831639.

COTSWOLD CANALS TRUST - Trips at Saul Junction (Map 28) Tel: 07929 980670 and Lechlade (Map 39) Tel: 01446 760314.

COTSWOLD RIVER CRUISES - Trips at Lechlade on the Upper Thames. Tel: 01793 574499.

GLOUCESTER LEISURE CRUISES - Trips from Gloucester Docks, Map 25. Tel: 01452 318200.

HANDSAM BOAT CO - River trips from Evesham, Map 4. Tel: 01386 834070 or 07860 895416.

RIVER SEVERN CRUISES - River trips from Worcester, Map 20. Tel: 01905 611060.

SALTERS - Scheduled services from Oxford southwards on the Thames, Map 45. Tel: 01865 243421.

SEVERN LEISURE CRUISES - Trips from Upton-on-Severn, Map 23. Tel: 01684 593112.

TELESTAR - River trips on the Avon from Tewkesbury. Tel: 01684 294088.

Acknowledgements

Special thanks to all at Bidford Boats on the River Avon. Brian Collings designed and executed the front cover. Thanks also to Toby Bryant of Central Waterways Supplies; Jackie, Tamar, and Eden Pearson, Tom Lumsden; and Karen Tanguy. Thanks to all at Hawksworths of Uttoxeter. Mapping reproduced by permission of Ordnance Survey (based mapping) on behalf of The Controller of Her Majesty's Stationary Office, Crown copyright 100033032.

Frontispiece - the Severn at Wainlode Hill
Back cover - Bidford-on-Avon

Healing's barges, Tewkesbury

Nine Good Reasons for Exploring the Canals with Pearsons

7th edition - ISBN 0 9545383 9 0

8th edition - ISBN 0 9549116 0 1

7th edition - ISBN 0 9549116 3 6

7th edition - ISBN 0 9545383 8 2

6th edition - ISBN 0 9549116 5 2

6th edition - ISBN 0 9545383 1 5

6th edition - ISBN 0 9549116 2 8

3rd edition - ISBN 0 9545383 4 X

1st edition - ISBN 0 907864 97 X

Pearson's Canal Companions are published by Central Waterways Supplies. They are widely available from hire bases, boatyards, canal shops, good bookshops, via the internet and the Inland Waterways Association. For further details contact CWS on 01788 546692 or sales@centralwaterways.co.uk